The National Science Foundation

The National Science Foundation

Patricia L. Barnes-Svarney

CHELSEA HOUSE PUBLISHERS

Chelsea House Publishers
Editor-in-Chief: Nancy Toff
Executive Editor: Remmel T. Nunn
Managing Editor: Karyn Gullen Browne
Copy Chief: Juliann Barbato
Picture Editor: Adrian G. Allen
Art Director: Maria Epes
Manufacturing Manager: Gerald Levine

Know Your Government
Senior Editor: Kathy Kuhtz

Staff for THE NATIONAL SCIENCE FOUNDATION
Associate Editor: Pierre Hauser
Deputy Copy Chief: Ellen Scordato
Editorial Assistant: Elizabeth Nix
Picture Researchers: Ed Dixon, Michele Brisson
Assistant Art Director: Laurie Jewell
Senior Designer: Noreen M. Lamb
Production Coordinator: Joseph Romano

First Printing

1 3 5 7 9 8 6 4 2

Library of Congress Cataloging-in-Publication Data

Barnes-Svarney, Patricia.
    The National Science Foundation.

    (Know your government)
    Bibliography: p.
    Includes index.
    Summary: Surveys the history of the National Science Foundation, describing its structure,
function, and influence on American society.
    1. National Science Foundation (U.S.)—Juvenile literature. [1. National Science Foundation
(U.S.)] I. Title. II. Series: Know your government (New York, N.Y.)
Q11.B26   1989   353.0085'5   88-25766
ISBN 1-55546-117-4
        0-7910-0870-3 (pbk.)

CONTENTS

KNOW YOUR GOVERNMENT

CHELSEA HOUSE PUBLISHERS

INTRODUCTION

Government: Crises of Confidence

Arthur M. Schlesinger, jr.

From the start, Americans have regarded their government with a mixture of reliance and mistrust. The men who founded the republic did not doubt the indispensability of government. "If men were angels," observed the 51st Federalist Paper, "no government would be necessary." But men are not angels. Because human beings are subject to wicked as well as to noble impulses, government was deemed essential to assure freedom and order.

At the same time, the American revolutionaries knew that government could also become a source of injury and oppression. The men who gathered in Philadelphia in 1787 to write the Constitution therefore had two purposes in mind. They wanted to establish a strong central authority and to limit that central authority's capacity to abuse its power.

To prevent the abuse of power, the Founding Fathers wrote two basic principles into the new Constitution. The principle of federalism divided power between the state governments and the central authority. The principle of the separation of powers subdivided the central authority itself into three branches—the executive, the legislative, and the judiciary—so that "each may be a check on the other." The *Know Your Government* series focuses on the major executive departments and agencies in these branches of the federal government.

7

The Constitution did not plan the executive branch in any detail. After vesting the executive power in the president, it assumed the existence of "executive departments" without specifying what these departments should be. Congress began defining their functions in 1789 by creating the Departments of State, Treasury, and War. The secretaries in charge of these departments made up President Washington's first cabinet. Congress also provided for a legal officer, and President Washington soon invited the attorney general, as he was called, to attend cabinet meetings. As need required, Congress created more executive departments.

Setting up the cabinet was only the first step in organizing the American state. With almost no guidance from the Constitution, President Washington, seconded by Alexander Hamilton, his brilliant secretary of the treasury, equipped the infant republic with a working administrative structure. The Federalists believed in both executive energy and executive accountability and set high standards for public appointments. The Jeffersonian opposition had less faith in strong government and preferred local government to the central authority. But when Jefferson himself became president in 1801, although he set out to change the direction of policy, he found no reason to alter the framework the Federalists had erected.

By 1801 there were about 3,000 federal civilian employees in a nation of a little more than 5 million people. Growth in territory and population steadily enlarged national responsibilities. Thirty years later, when Jackson was president, there were more than 11,000 government workers in a nation of 13 million. The federal establishment was increasing at a faster rate than the population.

Jackson's presidency brought significant changes in the federal service. He believed that the executive branch contained too many officials who saw their jobs as "species of property" and as "a means of promoting individual interest." Against the idea of a permanent service based on life tenure, Jackson argued for the periodic redistribution of federal offices, contending that this was the democratic way and that official duties could be made "so plain and simple that men of intelligence may readily qualify themselves for their performance." He called this policy rotation-in-office. His opponents called it the spoils system.

In fact, partisan legend exaggerated the extent of Jackson's removals. More than 80 percent of federal officeholders retained their jobs. Jackson discharged no larger a proportion of government workers than Jefferson had done a generation earlier. But the rise in these years of mass political parties gave federal patronage new importance as a means of building the party and of rewarding activists. Jackson's successors were less restrained in the distribu-

8

tion of spoils. As the federal establishment grew—to nearly 40,000 by 1861—the politicization of the public service excited increasing concern.

After the Civil War the spoils system became a major political issue. High-minded men condemned it as the root of all political evil. The spoilsmen, said the British commentator James Bryce, "have distorted and depraved the mechanism of politics." Patronage, by giving jobs to unqualified, incompetent, and dishonest persons, lowered the standards of public service and nourished corrupt political machines. Office-seekers pursued presidents and cabinet secretaries without mercy. "Patronage," said Ulysses S. Grant after his presidency, "is the bane of the presidential office." "Every time I appoint someone to office," said another political leader, "I make a hundred enemies and one ingrate." George William Curtis, the president of the National Civil Service Reform League, summed up the indictment. He said,

> The theory which perverts public trusts into party spoils, making public
> employment dependent upon personal favor and not on proved merit,
> necessarily ruins the self-respect of public employees, destroys the
> function of party in a republic, prostitutes elections into a desperate
> strife for personal profit, and degrades the national character by lower-
> ing the moral tone and standard of the country.

The object of civil service reform was to promote efficiency and honesty in the public service and to bring about the ethical regeneration of public life. Over bitter opposition from politicians, the reformers in 1883 passed the Pendleton Act, establishing a bipartisan Civil Service Commission, competitive examinations, and appointment on merit. The Pendleton Act also gave the president authority to extend by executive order the number of "classified" jobs—that is, jobs subject to the merit system. The act applied initially only to about 14,000 of the more than 100,000 federal positions. But by the end of the 19th century 40 percent of federal jobs had moved into the classified category.

Civil service reform was in part a response to the growing complexity of American life. As society grew more organized and problems more technical, official duties were no longer so plain and simple that any person of intelligence could perform them. In public service, as in other areas, the all-round man was yielding ground to the expert, the amateur to the professional. The excesses of the spoils system thus provoked the counter-ideal of scientific public administration, separate from politics and, as far as possible, insulated against it.

The cult of the expert, however, had its own excesses. The idea that administration could be divorced from policy was an illusion. And in the realm of policy, the expert, however much segregated from partisan politics, can never attain perfect objectivity. He remains the prisoner of his own set of values. It is these values rather than technical expertise that determine fundamental judgments of public policy. To turn over such judgments to experts, moreover, would be to abandon democracy itself; for in a democracy final decisions must be made by the people and their elected representatives. "The business of the expert," the British political scientist Harold Laski rightly said, "is to be on tap and not on top."

Politics, however, were deeply ingrained in American folkways. This meant intermittent tension between the presidential government, elected every four years by the people, and the permanent government, which saw presidents come and go while it went on forever. Sometimes the permanent government knew better than its political masters; sometimes it opposed or sabotaged valuable new initiatives. In the end a strong president with effective cabinet secretaries could make the permanent government responsive to presidential purpose, but it was often an exasperating struggle.

The struggle within the executive branch was less important, however, than the growing impatience with bureaucracy in society as a whole. The 20th century saw a considerable expansion of the federal establishment. The Great Depression and the New Deal led the national government to take on a variety of new responsibilities. The New Deal extended the federal regulatory apparatus. By 1940, in a nation of 130 million people, the number of federal workers for the first time passed the 1 million mark. The Second World War brought federal civilian employment to 3.8 million in 1945. With peace, the federal establishment declined to around 2 million by 1950. Then growth resumed, reaching 2.8 million by the 1980s.

The New Deal years saw rising criticism of "big government" and "bureaucracy." Businessmen resented federal regulation. Conservatives worried about the impact of paternalistic government on individual self-reliance, on community responsibility, and on economic and personal freedom. The nation in effect renewed the old debate between Hamilton and Jefferson in the early republic, although with an ironic exchange of positions. For the Hamiltonian constituency, the "rich and well-born," once the advocate of affirmative government, now condemned government intervention, while the Jeffersonian constituency, the plain people, once the advocate of a weak central government and of states' rights, now favored government intervention.

In the 1980s, with the presidency of Ronald Reagan, the debate has burst out with unusual intensity. According to conservatives, government intervention abridges liberty, stifles enterprise, and is inefficient, wasteful, and arbitrary. It disturbs the harmony of the self-adjusting market and creates worse troubles than it solves. Get government off our backs, according to the popular cliché, and our problems will solve themselves. When government is necessary, let it be at the local level, close to the people. Above all, stop the inexorable growth of the federal government.

In fact, for all the talk about the "swollen" and "bloated" bureaucracy, the federal establishment has not been growing as inexorably as many Americans seem to believe. In 1949, it consisted of 2.1 million people. Thirty years later, while the country had grown by 70 million, the federal force had grown only by 750,000. Federal workers were a smaller percentage of the population in 1985 than they were in 1955—or in 1940. The federal establishment, in short, has not kept pace with population growth. Moreover, national defense and the postal service account for 60 percent of federal employment.

Why then the widespread idea about the remorseless growth of government? It is partly because in the 1960s the national government assumed new and intrusive functions: affirmative action in civil rights, environmental protection, safety and health in the workplace, community organization, legal aid to the poor. Although this enlargement of the federal regulatory role was accompanied by marked growth in the size of government on all levels, the expansion has taken place primarily in state and local government. Whereas the federal force increased by only 27 percent in the 30 years after 1950, the state and local government force increased by an astonishing 212 percent.

Despite the statistics, the conviction flourishes in some minds that the national government is a steadily growing behemoth swallowing up the liberties of the people. The foes of Washington prefer local government, feeling it is closer to the people and therefore allegedly more responsive to popular needs. Obviously there is a great deal to be said for settling local questions locally. But local government is characteristically the government of the locally powerful. Historically, the way the locally powerless have won their human and constitutional rights has often been through appeal to the national government. The national government has vindicated racial justice against local bigotry, defended the Bill of Rights against local vigilantism, and protected natural resources against local greed. It has civilized industry and secured the rights of labor organizations. Had the states' rights creed prevailed, there would perhaps still be slavery in the United States.

The national authority, far from diminishing the individual, has given most Americans more personal dignity and liberty than ever before. The individual freedoms destroyed by the increase in national authority have been in the main the freedom to deny black Americans their rights as citizens; the freedom to put small children to work in mills and immigrants in sweatshops; the freedom to pay starvation wages, require barbarous working hours, and permit squalid working conditions; the freedom to deceive in the sale of goods and securities; the freedom to pollute the environment—all freedoms that, one supposes, a civilized nation can readily do without.

"Statements are made," said President John F. Kennedy in 1963, "labelling the Federal Government an outsider, an intruder, an adversary. . . . The United States Government is not a stranger or not an enemy. It is the people of fifty states joining in a national effort. . . . Only a great national effort by a great people working together can explore the mysteries of space, harvest the products at the bottom of the ocean, and mobilize the human, natural, and material resources of our lands."

So an old debate continues. However, Americans are of two minds. When pollsters ask large, spacious questions—Do you think government has become too involved in your lives? Do you think government should stop regulating business?—a sizable majority opposes big government. But when asked specific questions about the practical work of government—Do you favor social security? unemployment compensation? Medicare? health and safety standards in factories? environmental protection? government guarantee of jobs for everyone seeking employment? price and wage controls when inflation threatens?—a sizable majority approves of intervention.

In general, Americans do not want less government. What they want is more efficient government. They want government to do a better job. For a time in the 1970s, with Vietnam and Watergate, Americans lost confidence in the national government. In 1964, more than three-quarters of those polled had thought the national government could be trusted to do right most of the time. By 1980 only one-quarter was prepared to offer such trust. But by 1984 trust in the federal government to manage national affairs had climbed back to 45 percent.

Bureaucracy is a term of abuse. But it is impossible to run any large organization, whether public or private, without a bureaucracy's division of labor and hierarchy of authority. And we live in a world of large organizations. Without bureaucracy modern society would collapse. The problem is not to abolish bureaucracy, but to make it flexible, efficient, and capable of innovation.

Two hundred years after the drafting of the Constitution, Americans still regard government with a mixture of reliance and mistrust—a good combination. Mistrust is the best way to keep government reliable. Informed criticism

12

is the means of correcting governmental inefficiency, incompetence, and arbitrariness; that is, of best enabling government to play its essential role. For without government, we cannot attain the goals of the Founding Fathers. Without an understanding of government, we cannot have the informed criticism that makes government do the job right. It is the duty of every American citizen to know our government—which is what this series is all about.

*A blue-footed booby performs a mating ritual on the Galapagos Is-
lands. The Galapagos archipelago, a group of rocky volcanic islands
that lie about 600 miles off the western coast of Ecuador, provides scientists with a natural laboratory to study wildlife and the effects of
volcanic eruptions on the islands' ecological communities. To encourage study of the islands, the NSF provides funding for the Galapagos
International Scientific Project.*

ONE

The Importance of Funding Science

The Galapagos archipelago is a collection of strange and beautiful islands. Situated amid a field of active volcanoes off the coast of South America, the islands are home to a remarkable variety of plant and animal species—some of which are indigenous to the area, others of which strayed there during migrations and adapted to the islands' cool and dry climate. The islands' flora and fauna are becoming ever more diverse as upheavals in the local geology continue. Each time a volcano erupts, the islands in the shadow of the explosion are blanketed with a new layer of dust, ash, and rock, which often wipes out part of the existing ecological community and gives rise to a new one. Over the years, the islands have served as a living laboratory for several generations of zoologists, vulcanologists, evolutionary biologists, and other scientists. In 1835, the British naturalist Charles Darwin visited the islands, making observations of island wildlife that helped inspire his theories of natural selection. Today, study of the islands continues under the Galapagos International Science Project.

Across the Pacific Ocean from the Galapagos Islands is another area of interest to scientists—the geological system that underlies the islands of Japan. During the 20th century, Japan has experienced more large earthquakes than any other area in the world. Currently, researchers from the United States–

Townspeople flee the smoky haze during an earthquake's destruction of a city in Japan. The NSF supports a U.S.-Japanese study to predict earthquakes in an effort to minimize property damage and save lives.

Japan Seminar on Earthquake Precursors are hard at work trying to develop a method of predicting these violent natural events so as to minimize damage to buildings and people.

The earthquake project and the Galapagos International Science Project are only two of many current scientific research projects that owe their existence to funding from the National Science Foundation (NSF). Over the past four decades, the NSF has constantly been on the cutting edge of scientific discovery. It has supported biological research to unravel the mysteries of cold viruses and astronomical studies to view galaxies that formed billions of years ago. It has also promoted studies to develop a supercomputer and to build a microscope that can display the world of atoms.

What is this organization that does so much to promote the advancement of scientific knowledge? The NSF is a federal agency whose primary function is to distribute government funds to support scientific research. It allots money in the form of grants and contracts to scientists affiliated with universities, private companies, and other government departments. It is not the only federal agency that funds scientific research. The Department of Defense spends billions of dollars a year on weapons development, and the National Institutes of Health pay for a wide array of medical research projects. But the NSF is the only agency whose primary task is funding research. It is the only one that conducts no research of its own. It is the only one that funds research in all scientific disciplines. And it is the only one that devotes most of its attention to basic research—research "performed without thought of practical ends," in the words of Vannevar Bush, a scientific adviser to President Franklin D. Roosevelt during the 1940s.

The vast majority of grants awarded by the NSF are for "little science" projects—that is, research conducted by individual academic scientists with the assistance of one or two graduate students. Little science projects usually have specific goals and run for a fixed period of time. But the NSF has also backed several "big science" projects—projects that require tremendous expenditures on equipment, involve a considerable number of scientists, and run indefinitely. Most of the foundation's big science projects are in the fields of astronomy and atmospheric research, disciplines that call for facilities that most private institutions cannot possibly afford to build and operate. The NSF has established a number of permanent installations for astronomical research—including the Kitt Peak National Observatory near Tucson, Arizona, and the National Radio Astronomy Observatory in Green Bank, West Virginia. It is, however, prohibited by its charter from actually running the centers, so it hires associations of universities to operate them. The Galapagos International Science Project and the United States–Japan Seminar on Earthquake Precursors are examples of big science projects.

A scientist experiments with robotics—a technology dealing with the design, construction, and operation of robots in automation. The majority of NSF grants are awarded to small-scale science projects, whose research team usually consists of no more than an individual academic scientist and one or two research assistants.

17

An exhibit on static electricity at a local science fair arouses a young boy's curiosity. The NSF seeks to improve precollege science instruction by funding institutes that train teachers and by developing new curricula in physics, biology, chemistry, and mathematics.

Although funding research is its main duty, the NSF also does much to support education in the sciences on all levels. Every year it awards thousands of graduate fellowships, stipends that help graduate students in the sciences pay for their education; seeks to improve precollege science programs by funding institutes that train teachers and by sponsoring efforts to develop new curricula in physics, biology, chemistry, and mathematics; and also provides university science departments with grants to purchase laboratory supplies and strengthen graduate and undergraduate instruction.

The NSF has two other important tasks—sponsoring international scientific cooperation and disseminating information on the sciences. It arranges for exchanges of scientists between the United States and other nations, represents the United States at international conferences, and sets up joint research endeavors with other countries. Maintaining a massive bank of data on recent scientific discoveries, distributing information on sources of funding for the sciences, maintaining a register of personnel involved in science, and publishing scientific periodicals are all part of its efforts to circulate scientific information.

The NSF is headed by a director, who manages day-to-day activities, and the 25-member National Science Board, a panel of scientists and educators that meets several times a year to formulate foundation policy. In an arrangement that is unusual among federal agencies, the director and the board share power equally. The NSF has status as an *independent agency*. This term is somewhat of a misnomer in that the NSF, like all other executive bodies, remains dependent on Congress for funding and on the president for direction. The term simply means that the foundation is not subordinate to an existing federal department or bureau. It should be noted that the foundation is *not* involved in formulating national science policy. In other words, it does not determine the goals of the government as a whole in the sciences, and it does not coordinate the activities of all federal agencies involved in science. Since 1962, those responsibilities have belonged to the Office of Science and Technology, a branch of the Executive Office of the President.

The NSF was established in 1950 after a long debate in Congress over what its role should be. Since then, it has seen considerable growth and change. Between 1950 and 1988, its budget grew from $250,000 to $1.9 billion. During that period, it paid increasing attention to funding big science projects and applied research—research with specific, practical aims. Its educational programs were also expanded. But today its goals remain the same as when it was founded—to promote national growth and help the nation remain a leader in scientific progress by channeling funds into scientific research and education.

A 19th-century illustration depicts Benjamin Franklin performing his famous kite experiment. Franklin attached a key to the string of a kite during a lightning storm to prove that electricity manufactured in a laboratory is the same force as that produced in a storm.

TWO

The Origins of the NSF

The NSF has been in existence only since 1950. But the federal government has been involved in promoting the advancement of scientific knowledge almost since the country was established. Over the course of the nation's first century and a half, the government set up several organizations that conducted and supported scientific research. Unlike the NSF, each of these agencies was involved in only one or two disciplines and each was primarily concerned with the practical applications of discoveries. Yet the government's experience with these agencies strongly influenced Congress in formulating the legislation that established the NSF.

The Nation's First Scientists

Many of the founding fathers of the United States took an avid interest in science, and some were themselves inventors and scientists. In addition to being a successful statesman, diplomat, publisher, and writer, Benjamin Franklin made numerous scientific discoveries. In 1740, at the age of 32, he

The polygraph, invented by Thomas Jefferson, consists of a mechanical arm to which a writer can attach his pen while producing a document. The mechanical arm is able to duplicate the movement of the writer's pen to create a second, nearly identical document.

conceived his first invention, a heating stove that greatly improved upon existing models. In later years, Franklin invented bifocal lenses, designed ships, tracked storm paths, and formulated a theory of heat absorption. His most significant investigations involved electricity. In 1752, using a procedure designed by Franklin, researchers in France determined that lightning was a form of electricity. That same year, he performed his most famous experiment. Flying a kite with a key attached to it during a lightning storm, Franklin demonstrated that static electricity produced in laboratories was the same force as that found in nature.

Another founding father, Thomas Jefferson, invented a copying device called the polygraph. The device consisted of a mechanical arm to which the user attached his pen while writing a document. The mechanical arm duplicated the movement of the user's pen to produce a second, nearly identical document. Jefferson was also one of the first Americans to study fossils. He housed his collection along with an extensive library of scientific books at Monticello, the estate he designed for himself in the Virginia countryside.

Jefferson, Franklin, and other early American leaders realized the importance of scientific knowledge to the development of the country. During the Constitutional Convention of 1787, they discussed the possibility of using the Constitution to assign the federal government a prominent role in the promotion of scientific research. In the end, however, they decided not to mention the issue in the governing document. The only passage in the Constitution that refers to science empowers Congress to protect inventions from being copied. It reads, "Congress is to promote the Progress of Science and useful Arts, by securing for limited Times to Authors and Inventors the exclusive right to their respective Writings and Discoveries."

The nation's first president, George Washington, was too preoccupied with the difficult task of establishing a new nation to pay any attention to the issue of science. The federal government's only science-related action during his presidency was the passage of laws concerning patents (documents that confer on their holder the sole right to make and sell an invention). Under the third American president, Thomas Jefferson, the government made its first financial contribution to the expansion of scientific knowledge. After convincing France

Commander John Wilkes drew this sketch of Antarctica during his 1838 exploration of the continent. The Wilkes expedition, which was undertaken to survey and chart areas of the Pacific Ocean and the South Seas, was the first federally funded mapping mission that involved professional scientists.

A scientist-explorer records information about the shoreline of the Colorado River in 1871. Although Colorado did not achieve statehood until 1918, the federal government had already sponsored several expeditions to its western territories, beginning with Lewis and Clark's 1804 exploration of the Rocky Mountain region and Zebulon Pike's 1806 exploration of the headwaters of the Arkansas River.

to sell the United States a massive tract of land west of the Mississippi in 1803 (a transaction known as the Louisiana Purchase), Jefferson commissioned two exploratory missions to the area to investigate its geography, geology, wildlife, and Indian populations. In 1804, Jefferson sent Meriwether Lewis and William Clark to explore the headwaters of the Missouri River and Rocky Mountains. And in 1806, he dispatched Zebulon Pike, a lieutenant in the U.S. Army, to explore land near present-day Colorado. Jefferson also convinced Congress to fund the Coast Survey, a charting of the geography of the East Coast of the United States.

Over the next half-century, the government sponsored several additional explorations of the American frontier and beyond. In 1838, it funded John Wilkes's expedition to Antarctica. The Wilkes expedition, known officially as the United States Exploring Expedition to Antarctica, was the first mission funded by the federal government that involved professional scientists. State governments also sponsored efforts to explore America. By 1850, most states had established geological surveys, agencies that hired scientists and explorers to map the state's territories and study its geology. In 1879, Congress would set up such an agency at the federal level, the U.S. Geological Survey (USGS).

The Nation's First Science Agencies

In 1846, Congress created an unusual quasi-governmental organization called the Smithsonian Institution. Part of its mission was to conduct and support scientific research, preserve scientific items for study and reference, and display scientific exhibits in its museums. The organization was the product of the generosity of James Smithson, a British nobleman who dabbled in mineralogy and chemistry. In 1829, Smithson died, inexplicably leaving all of his quite substantial fortune to the United States to found "under the name Smithsonian Institution, an establishment for the increase and diffusion of knowledge among men." At first, Congress considered renouncing the bequest because it was thought to be an example of British condescension. But after years of debating how to use the funds, in 1846 the lawmakers agreed to use the money to promote research in science and the arts and to house "all objects of art and of foreign and curious research, and all objects of natural history, plants, and genealogical and mineralogical specimens, belonging or hereafter to belong to the United States."

Under its first head, the physicist Joseph Henry, the Smithsonian directed most of its resources toward science. During Henry's 33-year term, the organization acquired a wealth of scientific specimens, launched several science

A late-19th-century photograph of the Smithsonian Institution in Washington, D.C. The Smithsonian was established in 1846 after British scientist James Smithson bequeathed his fortune to the United States for the purpose of promoting research. Over the years, the Smithsonian has developed a network of art and science museums and has funded a variety of important science projects.

publications, and set up an office to receive meteorological reports by telegraph from around the country. He also hired a team of amateur scientists to conduct studies on the size and shape of the United States. Ultimately, Henry made the Smithsonian the center of American science during the second half of the 19th century.

After Henry's departure, the Smithsonian would seek greater balance between its scientific and artistic programs. But the organization would eventually establish several major scientific centers, including the Astrophysical Smithsonian Observatory in Cambridge, Massachusetts; the Smithsonian Environmental Research Center in Edgewater, Maryland; and the Smithsonian Tropical Research Center in the Panama Canal Zone. In funding various kinds of scientific research, the Smithsonian came close to serving the same purpose that the NSF would eventually fill. But in other ways the Smithsonian differed

26

from the NSF—in its use of both private and federal funds, in that it supported both science and art, and in that it did not address all scientific disciplines.

With the Smithsonian playing a prominent role, American science grew rapidly during the second half of the 19th century. Prior to that time, the country had few professional scientists, and most people involved in research pursued it as a hobby or second career. However, by the Civil War, professional scientists constituted a distinct and growing segment of society. The majority of scientists were employed by academic institutions. But the emergence of several science-related industries during the late 19th century, such as the electrical and chemical industries, created additional employment opportunities.

Alexander Graham Bell operates the telephone, a machine that he invented in 1876. Prior to the Civil War most scientists could not make a living in their own field; however, with the establishment of the Smithsonian Institution and the growing need for scientists by academic institutions and the electrical and chemical industries, more employment opportunities opened up, promoting scientific research and technological progress.

A scientist in the U.S. Department of Agriculture studies the effects different climates have on the same plant. Since its creation in 1862, the USDA has sponsored such investigations in an effort to help farmers increase crop production.

The rapid increase in the number of scientists was paralleled by a proliferation of scientific societies. A number of societies with a fairly general focus had been established during the 1700s—notably the American Philosophical Society (1744) and the American Academy of Arts and Sciences (1780). In the 19th century, they were joined by several more specialized societies—the American Chemical Society (1876), the Geological Society of America (1888), and the Boston Society of Natural History (1830). By mid-century, science courses were part of most universities' programs. In the 1840s, several prominent schools were established for higher education in the sciences, including the Lawrence Scientific School at Harvard and the Sheffield Scientific School at Yale. The Massachusetts Institute of Technology (MIT), a science and engineering school, was founded in 1861. Following a tradition—established in Germany—of connecting education and research, many American universities set up research laboratories.

During the Civil War, federal leaders increased ties with the burgeoning scientific community. In 1863, Congress established the National Academy of Sciences, an honorary organization for distinguished scientists. Although chartered by the federal government, the academy was officially a private institution. Its main activities were issuing science publications and holding regular meetings for the discussion of scientific topics. In addition, the academy was assigned to advise the federal government on scientific and technical matters and to help the government hire scientific personnel.

Also during the Civil War, Congress established the Department of Agriculture (USDA), the first full-fledged government agency to become involved in scientific research. (The Smithsonian and the Academy of Sciences were both semiprivate.) Although today the USDA devotes most of its resources to providing financial assistance to farmers, in its early years it concentrated heavily on developing new agricultural technologies. In its first year of operation, the department set up several research bureaus, including one that studied the raising and breeding of animals. Under the 1887 Hatch Act, the department began funding agricultural experiment stations (consisting of farmlands and laboratories) at colleges around the nation.

In the first two decades of the 20th century, the federal government set up several additional agencies that concerned themselves in one way or another with science. The Bureau of Mines was established in 1910 to develop new technologies for extracting, processing, and using nonfuel mineral resources. The Public Health Service was established in 1912 to conduct medical research, operate quarantine stations (posts where ships were detained in isolation), run hospitals for merchant seamen, and deal with public health emergencies. And the National Advisory Committee for Aeronautics was created in 1915 to assist university engineering departments in expanding knowledge about the principles of flight. But each of these agencies dealt with only one small piece of the scientific picture. Each was interested only in projects with practical applications. As J. Stefan Dupré and Sanford A. Laskoff have written in their book *Science and the Nation: Policy and Politics*, the federal government regarded science "not as a thing apart, valuable in itself, but always and only as a tool for the solution of problems and the formulation of policy." There was still no agency assigned to promote research in all disciplines or to articulate a national science policy.

During World War I, scientific research took on increasing importance to federal leaders because of the central role new technology played in the hostilities. The wartime president, Woodrow Wilson, set up the National Research Council (NRC) to conduct research in the areas of gas warfare and optics. He also increased government cooperation with private scientists through a new agency called the Naval Consulting Board. Established in 1915 under the supervision of the inventor Thomas Edison, the board hired hundreds of private scientists to serve on committees that advised the government on weapons development.

Science was given low priority by the government during the 1920s. In an attempt to limit government interference in the economy, Presidents Warren Harding and Calvin Coolidge convinced Congress to reduce spending on many domestic programs, including science programs. The NRC and the Naval Consulting Board were hit especially hard by the cuts. In the words of Dupré and Laskoff, "America kept cool with Coolidge . . . and science was relegated to the proverbial ivory tower." When Herbert Hoover, a former mining engineer, became president in 1929, he tried to set up a national fund for scientific research, supported by contributions from major corporations. But business leaders were reluctant to spend money on a seemingly nonessential program amid the economic turmoil of the Great Depression.

FDR: A New Approach to Science

Franklin D. Roosevelt, elected president in 1932, fundamentally altered the government's approach to science. In 1933, by executive order, he established the Science Advisory Board, which was the first federal agency to deal with a wide spectrum of scientific disciplines. The board consisted of a panel of privately employed scientists who prepared reports for the president on the

Engineers from the Bureau of Mines plan a mining operation in a specially designed safety car. The bureau was established in 1910 to develop new technologies for extracting, processing, and using non-fuel mineral resources.

progress of research projects conducted by the various federal science organizations. It had only a brief life. In 1935, it issued a detailed report on federal science programs in which it urged Congress to increase federal spending for research and reduce government control. Lawmakers were offended by the suggestion that the government should stay out of scientific policy. After two and a half years, Congress decided that the money being allocated to the board would be better spent on combating economic problems, and the board was disbanded.

In 1941, Roosevelt established a second science organization with a broad focus, the Office of Scientific Research and Development (OSRD). It was assigned to coordinate efforts to develop military technology for use by American forces in World War II. It supervised weapons research by other federal agencies, conducted research of its own, funded research by the private sector, served as a clearinghouse for information on new technology, and mobilized scientific manpower for the government. It developed several new weapons, including a rocket-launching bazooka and radar that could detect antiaircraft fire. For each of its inventions, it produced a prototype ready for manufacture. Within the OSRD, the task of funding private research was delegated to a subdivision called the National Defense Research Committee. Members of the committee included the U.S. commissioner of patents, the president of Bell Telephone, a general, an admiral, and two university scientists. Much of the OSRD's research money went to universities and private companies to set up research centers. The best known of these was the Los Alamos laboratory, where physicist J. R. Oppenheimer directed the design and manufacture of the first atomic weapons.

The OSRD was headed by Vannevar Bush, the former dean of engineering at MIT and the president of the Carnegie Institution in Washington, D.C. Bush used his extensive contacts in the scientific community to assemble an exceptional staff. The scientists he recruited included James Conant, a chemist who was the president of Harvard, and Karl T. Compton, the president of MIT. Many of the nation's academic scientists heeded Bush's call to become involved in military research after seeing their university classes depleted by the draft. Most plunged wholeheartedly into the task of developing scientific knowledge in order to defeat the nation's enemies, seeing it as a noble cause. A number of scientists who did not themselves conduct research for the government served on advisory committees. Ultimately, Bush brought "almost the entire scientific community into close cooperation with the government in one way or another," in the words of Dorothy Schaffter, a specialist on American government for the Library of Congress.

Engineers inspect radar equipment developed by the Office of Scientific Research and Development (OSRD). Established by President Franklin D. Roosevelt in 1941, the OSRD took on the task of improving military technology, developing new weapons, and supervising weapons research by other federal agencies to better arm American forces in World War II.

An OSRD scientist studies cultures containing radioactive compounds at the Los Alamos laboratory in New Mexico. At the same laboratory the physicist J. Robert Oppenheimer directed the design and manufacture of the first atomic bomb.

Vannevar Bush was appointed head of the OSRD in 1941. Bush, who was also President Roosevelt's chief science adviser, prepared a highly influential report, Science: The Endless Frontier, *in which he supported a central coordinating agency for science and technology that would replace the OSRD.*

Bush was able to win tremendous power for his agency. Because the OSRD was attached to the Executive Office of the President, Bush had direct access to the president. He took advantage of this arrangement to secure for himself status as Roosevelt's principal science adviser. He was the first person ever to play such a role in the federal government. His influence with Roosevelt enabled Bush to ensure that the scientists he employed remained free from interference by government officials.

As the war drew to a close, it became clear that the OSRD would be disbanded when the hostilities ceased. But many federal leaders were so impressed with the OSRD's effectiveness in coordinating federal science activities that they began to examine the idea of establishing a comparable agency during peacetime. The first person to call for such an agency was Harley M. Kilgore, a liberal Democratic senator from West Virginia. At first Kilgore pushed his colleagues in Congress to establish a major department for science that would be responsible for establishing federal science policy and would be staffed by a career service of scientists that would include a considerable portion of the scientific community. When a majority of legislators rejected this idea, Kilgore modified his plan, proposing instead an agency that would fund and coordinate scientific research for nonmilitary purposes.

Senator Harley M. Kilgore of West Virginia proposed the creation of an agency that would replace the OSRD and would fund and coordinate scientific research for nonmilitary purposes. Kilgore believed that funding should be apportioned evenly among private and public colleges nationwide.

President Roosevelt also supported the idea of a central coordinating agency for science and technology and on November 17, 1944, wrote a letter to Vannevar Bush asking for his suggestions on setting up such an organization. In response, Bush wrote a report entitled *Science: The Endless Frontier,* in which he argued that "there should be a focal point within the government . . . to furnish the funds needed to support basic research in the colleges and universities, coordinate where possible research programs on matters of utmost importance to the national welfare, formulate a national policy for the government toward science, and sponsor the interchange of scientific information among scientists and laboratories both in this country and abroad." Bush recommended against giving such responsibilities to one of the government's existing science agencies because those agencies considered science to be "peripheral" to their major concerns. Such agencies, he argued, were "under constant pressure to produce in a tangible way," and therefore would tend to favor research with practical applications, to the detriment of purely speculative projects. Bush recommended instead the creation of what he called a "national research foundation." Bush's report was a seminal document. Though he was not the first person to call for a science foundation, he was the first to prepare a detailed study of the idea. And it was his report that prompted Congress to begin the discussions that ultimately led to the creation of the NSF. For these reasons, Bush is regarded as the founding father of the NSF.

The Long Debate

In the wake of Bush's report, the majority of lawmakers agreed that a federal agency to support all types of scientific research was a good idea. But there was much disagreement on specific issues regarding its role and organization. It took more than five years of heated debate to resolve these issues. The debate focused on five questions: Should patents on inventions arising from research funded by the science foundation belong to the government or to the scientists? Should research funds be evenly distributed geographically? Should agency funds be made available to researchers in the social sciences? Should the agency focus on basic research or applied research? Who should have greater control over the agency, the scientific community or the government?

On several of these issues, Kilgore and Bush were at odds. For instance, whereas Bush favored allocating research funds only to the most prestigious universities in the Northeast, Kilgore wanted to apportion the money evenly among private and public colleges across the nation. On the issue of patents, Kilgore believed that all patents from government-funded research should become "the property of the United States, freely available for use by all taxpayers, not the property of individuals who could exploit publicly-paid-for discoveries for private gain," in the words of historian J. Merton England. Bush, in contrast, felt that private ownership of patents was necessary to provide incentive for innovative research.

Lawmakers fought most fiercely over the question of control of the foundation. One group wished to insulate the agency from partisan politics by putting it under the supervision of a board that would be appointed by the president but otherwise would function independently of the government. The other camp believed that the agency, like most federal departments, should be headed by a director who answered to the president. Members of the former group questioned the logic of entrusting the nation's scientific future to politicians and bureaucrats. Members of the latter group were aghast at the proposition that a public agency be put in the hands of private citizens.

The first two bills for a science research foundation were introduced on July 19, 1945, by Senator Warren G. Magnuson and Congressman Wilbur Mills. In the following two years these and several other similar bills were considered and rejected. Finally, in 1947, Congress passed a bill that would have established a central coordinating agency for science under the control of an independent board. The bill was vetoed, however, by President Harry S. Truman, who supported the creation of a science foundation but wanted it to be more accountable to the executive branch. In describing the reasons for his veto, Truman said, "The proposed National Science Foundation would be divorced from control by the people to an extent that implies a distinct lack of faith in the democratic process." In 1948 and 1949 both houses of Congress worked on bills to accommodate Truman's objections.

In the meantime, the idea of a science foundation received endorsement from two important executive bodies, an advisory committee called the Scientific Research Board and the Hoover Commission, a temporary panel formed in 1947 to examine ways of reorganizing the government. Both organizations issued reports that enriched the discussion of how the science foundation should be organized. The Scientific Research Board's report, entitled *A Program for the Nation*, urged the agency to play a strong role in supporting education, calling for it to develop "a program of assistance to undergraduate and graduate students in the sciences as an integral part of an overall national scholarship and fellowship program" and "a program of assistance to universities and colleges in the matters of laboratories and scientific equipment." The Hoover Commission, in a report issued in March 1949, recommended that the tasks of the science foundation be

> (a) to examine the total scientific research efforts of the Nation, (b) to assess the proper role of the Federal Government in this effort, (c) to evaluate the division of research efforts among the scientific disciplines and among fields of applied research, and (d) to evaluate the key factors that impede the development of an effective national research effort. Based upon its investigations, it should advise the President as to the measures necessary to establish a sound scientific research program for the Nation.

Another important event during the five-year congressional debate over a national science foundation was the establishment of a new federal science organization called the Office of Naval Research. This agency's primary purpose was limited—to fund and oversee research on weapons for use by the navy. But as a secondary task, it initiated the first federal program to fund basic research by university scientists. This program helped convince federal leaders of the value of supporting basic research. It also tested methods of administering grants that would later be employed by the NSF.

*On May 10, 1950, President Harry S. Truman (right) announced from
the rear platform of a railroad car in Pocatello, Idaho, that he had
signed the National Science Foundation Act. The bill granted the
NSF status as an independent agency.*

Establishment of the NSF

Congress finally passed the National Science Foundation bill on January 6, 1949. The lengthy deliberations on the measure enabled some members of Congress to become quite well informed about the agency they were creating. But the majority of lawmakers remained ignorant about the bill's fine points. Few understood that the law asked the NSF to fund basic research but not applied research. Had most lawmakers realized this, the debate would likely have lasted even longer than it did. The belief that the foundation would serve a practical purpose "did more than anything else to muster the votes needed for passage of the act," according to historian J. Merton England.

Although the bill reflected a clear-cut decision on the issue of applied versus basic research, it effected a compromise on, or sidestepped, the other issues that had caused disagreement in Congress. On the issue of control of the foundation, the bill compromised between those who wanted the NSF to be run by scientists and those who wanted it to be headed by bureaucrats. Power over the foundation was to be shared equally by a full-time director and a panel of scientists called the National Science Board. The president was charged with appointing the director and members of the board, subject to the consent of the Senate. To insulate the agency somewhat from political shifts, the director's term was set at six years. The bill left unresolved the social sciences issue. It did not specifically provide for social sciences, but by using the phrase "other sciences" it left the door open for NSF leaders to fund social sciences if they so chose. Similarly, on the question of geographic distribution, the bill required the NSF to avoid "undue concentration," but did not establish specific limits on the amount of research money a single university or region could receive. Lawmakers decided to ignore the patent question completely after realizing that few patentable inventions were likely to result from basic research.

On May 10, 1950, on the rear platform of a train in Pocatello, Idaho, Truman signed the bill officially establishing the NSF. It seemed an appropriate location in which to announce the formation of an organization dedicated to supporting scientific research because a century earlier it had served as a stopping place for the nation's first scientific researchers—explorers of the frontier. In approving the bill, Truman described the creation of the NSF as a watershed event in the history of the United States. By contributing to the advancement of scientific knowledge, he asserted, the NSF would play a key role in fostering national growth and prosperity. It would, he claimed further, help the country maintain its status as an international leader in scientific progress. He called upon all Americans to lend their support to the new agency.

Under the 1950 act, the NSF was given status as an independent agency. Its mission was to support scientific research and scientific education. More specifically, it was to perform the following tasks:

- Fund research in mathematics, physics, medicine, biology, engineering, and other sciences.
- Award college scholarships and graduate fellowships to students in the sciences.
- Promote the exchange of scientific information among scientists in the United States and foreign countries.
- Evaluate scientific research programs undertaken by other federal agencies and coordinate cooperation between those agencies and private researchers.
- Maintain a register of the nation's scientists and serve as a clearinghouse for information on the sciences.
- Initiate and fund a research program aimed at modifying weather in order to control such phenomena as floods, drought, lightning, fog, tornadoes, and hurricanes.

Alan Waterman, chief scientist in the Office of Naval Research, was named the first director of the NSF. Waterman found it difficult to convince Congress to allocate enough funds to the NSF to pay for the research grants and fellowships that the NSF deemed worthy of federal assistance.

THREE

Expanding Scientific Knowledge

By the time the NSF was created, the need for increased federal funding for the sciences had become acute. The cost of scientific research had risen phenomenally since the turn of the century, especially in the fields of particle physics, astronomy, and cosmology (the study of the nature of the universe), which required vast expenditures for equipment. In the years after World War II, a number of federal agencies had expanded their programs for scientific research. For instance, the National Institutes of Health, the research arm of the Public Health Service, had set up an array of new research institutes—the National Heart Institute, the National Institute of Dental Research, the National Microbiological Institute, and the Experimental Biological and Medical Institute—each of which allocated money to private researchers in addition to conducting its own studies. But more funds were sorely needed for basic research in several disciplines.

Choosing Leaders and Setting the Budget

Before the NSF could turn to the tasks of funding research and supporting science education, it had to set up an organizational structure. First, the

43

A researcher examines X rays at a National Institutes of Health (NIH) lab. After World War II, the NIH created a number of research institutes, such as the National Cancer Institute, to provide funding for private medical research and to improve NIH's own basic research programs.

president had to appoint the agency's leaders—a director and the National Science Board. In assembling the board, Truman had plenty of names from which to choose because his staff had been accumulating background information on potential candidates since the first NSF bill was sent to his office in 1947. He had to make sure each member met the qualifications spelled out in the act of 1950. The act required that members

> (1) shall be eminent in the fields of the basic sciences, medical science, engineering, agriculture, education, or public affairs; (2) shall be selected solely on the basis of established records of distinguished service; and (3) shall be so selected as to provide representation of the views of scientific leaders in all areas of the Nation.

Truman was also required by law to give due consideration to recommendations made by the scientific community. Even before the NSF act was passed, the National Academy of Sciences drew up a list of prospective board members. When the list was made public, it generated a great deal of controversy. Vannevar Bush criticized the academy for selecting too few candidates with experience in public affairs and education. In the months after Truman signed the NSF act, scientists across the nation vigorously debated the issue of board membership. They considered several questions: Should the board include an equal number of representatives from academia, government, and industry? Should minority scientists be given special consideration? Should assignments to the board be distributed evenly among geographic areas?

President Truman did as much as he could to respect the wishes of the scientific community, but in the end he had to make the decisions himself. He announced his choices on November 2, 1950. The 24 candidates included Sophie D. Aberle, special research director at the University of New Mexico; Chester I. Barnard, president of the Rockefeller Foundation; and Audrey A. Potter, dean of engineering at Purdue University. The group represented a

Twenty-one of the 24 members of the first National Science Board, in 1950. Seven of the members selected by President Truman were college or university presidents, 4 members were from companies that supported scientific research, and the other 13 members were university professors.

broad spectrum of backgrounds and specialties. All of the major scientific disciplines were represented; the geographic distribution of participants was mixed; and a considerable number of the candidates had experience in public affairs and education. The selections were applauded by most scientists, and all 24 were approved by the Senate.

Coming up with an acceptable candidate for NSF director proved a little more difficult. Truman's initial selection for the position was Frank P. Graham, a former senator from North Carolina who had recently lost a bid for reelection. Graham had a strong background in education, having served as president of the University of North Carolina, but his academic field was history, not science. Members of the newly created National Science Board resisted Graham's nomination, objecting to his lack of background in the sciences. They convinced Truman to abandon his choice and instead to look at a list of 10 candidates they themselves had compiled. At the top of the list was a member of the board, Detlev Bronk, who was the president of Johns Hopkins University. The Truman administration was disturbed by his professed desire to expand the foundation's authority and refused to consider him. The board's second choice, Alan T. Waterman, seemed the ideal candidate. Not only was he a respected physicist, but he had worked for several years for two government science organizations, the Office of Naval Research and the Office of Scientific Research and Development. Through his government jobs, he had become familiar with standard federal procedures for administering funds for scientific research, and as a scientist he understood the needs of the scientific community. On March 9, 1951, while on vacation in Key West, Florida, Truman sent a cable to the National Science Board, telling them that Waterman was his nominee. The board quickly approved the decision, as did the Senate.

The process of choosing NSF leaders had been slowed by the development of a major crisis overseas. On June 25, 1950, the communist government of North Korea had launched a surprise invasion of South Korea, starting the Korean War. The United States rallied to the defense of South Korea, an ally, and headed up a force of United Nations troops sent to the area to push the North Koreans back to their border, the 38th parallel. Preoccupied with organizing the American contribution to the war effort, Truman administration officials dragged their feet in establishing the NSF hierarchy.

The outbreak of war also affected efforts to establish the foundation's first budget. Soon after signing the NSF act, Truman requested that Congress allot $475,000 to the foundation for the fiscal year 1951. (The federal fiscal year is an accounting period that begins on October 1 of the year before the year for which it is named; hence, fiscal year 1951 ran from October 1, 1950, to

American soldiers capture a North Korean soldier during the Korean War. Throughout the early 1950s the NSF struggled to obtain sufficient funding from Congress to support basic research, but many congressmen thought the money allotted to the NSF budget could be better spent on the American war effort.

September 30, 1951.) At first Congress refused to appropriate any money at all to the NSF, arguing that the money should be spent instead on supplies for American troops in Korea. President Truman was disappointed, and NSF supporters were appalled. They pointed out to legislators that the NSF could be used to fund and coordinate weapons research and development during the conflict. After intensive lobbying by the scientific community, Congress finally

47

relented, agreeing to give the NSF $225,000. Truman approved the foundation's first budget on September 27, 1950.

Waterman's First Years

Alan Waterman was sworn in as director of the NSF on April 6, 1951. He would remain in that office for 12 years—the maximum length of time allowed. During that period, Waterman was the NSF's guiding spirit. Under his direction, the foundation would grow to become a major agency responsible for millions of dollars worth of research grants every year. But when he first assumed the position, the NSF was floundering. It had been in existence for more than a year, and it still had not undertaken its primary task—the distribution of funds for research. Waterman immediately set about putting the agency in working order. His first step was to fill the many openings that remained in its staff. In carrying out this duty, he took advantage of connections he had made during his previous service with government science agencies. He recruited heavily from the Office of Naval Research.

The next order of business for Waterman was to try to convince Congress to step up funding for the NSF. The $250,000 budget for fiscal year 1951 provided only enough money to cover organization and planning costs; it did not allocate funds for research grants. For fiscal year 1952, Waterman asked Congress to increase the budget to $8.6 million. Almost half of this figure was to pay for research grants in mathematics, physics, and engineering. Much of the rest was to pay for fellowships for graduate students in the sciences. As they had the year before, many members of Congress called for a complete halt to funding for the NSF. Again, many lawmakers argued that the money would be better spent on the American war effort in Korea. Others wanted to deny the foundation funds only temporarily, as a way of pressuring it to play a greater role in determining science policy—something Waterman had refused to do. In May 1952, Waterman attended numerous congressional hearings on the foundation's budget. Lawmakers used the occasion to rehash the old debate about the foundation's mission. Many wanted the NSF to serve a more practical purpose—to begin funding applied research on weapons for the war. In mid-August 1952, the House Appropriations Committee recommended that Congress allot only $300,000 to the foundation.

Waterman and his staff were outraged. With the assistance of Vannevar Bush and Brooks Hays, a Democratic congressman from Arkansas, they waged a vigorous campaign urging Congress to ignore the committee's recommendations. The *New York Times, Washington Post,* and other periodicals assisted, publishing editorials arguing that a financially healthy NSF was essential to scientific progress. It was a long, hard fight. But in October 1952, Congress agreed to appropriate $3.5 million for the foundation—much less than Waterman had asked for but enough for the NSF to begin supporting scientific research and education.

Waterman and the National Science Board had decided which scientists would receive the first batch of grants even before the 1952 budget was approved. (They had begun accepting grant applications soon after the NSF was established and had distributed guidelines to scientific institutions across the nation describing the proper form for research proposals.) In making this decision, NSF leaders had to draw heavily on the assistance of the scientific community. Each grant proposal was sent by mail to several reviewers and each was put before an advisory committee of scientists. At the insistence of Waterman, each was judged on the basis of the quality of the proposal and the

The Massachusetts Institute of Technology (MIT) in Cambridge, Massachusetts, received four grants from the NSF in 1952. Many of the early grants for projects went to individual researchers affiliated with prestigious universities such as Harvard, Yale, and MIT.

importance of the research—not on the basis of the applicant's institutional affiliations or political connections. Almost all of the grants were awarded for little science projects—small projects conducted by individual researchers at colleges and nonprofit organizations with the aid of research assistants. None of the grants went for big science projects—projects such as astronomical observatories that required large expenditures on equipment. All but two of the grants went to researchers affiliated with universities. Yale and MIT received the largest number of grants—four each.

Grant money was sent out soon after the NSF budget was approved. At the same time, the foundation began distributing college fellowships to graduate students. Prior to the budget fight, Waterman had hoped to award 2,000 fellowships in 1952, but congressional stinginess forced him to limit the number to a few hundred. As with research grants, fellowships were awarded on the basis of the quality of the application and the abilities of the applicant—not on politics. Recipients were allowed to use the money at any institution in the country, but most gravitated toward elite schools such as Harvard, Yale, and MIT. This trend caused resentment among institutions with less-established reputations and would later lead to reforms of NSF procedures.

Many of the practices instituted by Waterman and the NSF in awarding the first research grants and fellowships would be followed for many years thereafter. For instance, the focus on little science would continue until the late 1950s. The emphasis on quality remains in place today. In other ways, Waterman had a lasting impact on the NSF. For example, his refusal to let political considerations influence the foundation's actions has been continued by all of his successors. If a grant applicant was outspokenly critical of the Eisenhower administration, Waterman refused to disqualify him or her on that basis. In addition, Waterman initiated foundation efforts to compile and publish information on scientific research, established the foundation as an advocate for increased federal spending for research, and fostered strong ties between the NSF and the scientific community.

Many of the grants awarded in 1952 went toward studies that greatly advanced scientific knowledge. For instance, a $5,500 grant to Max Delbrueck, an MIT researcher, paid for a trailblazing study in the field of genetics. Called "Mechanism Underlying Genetic Recombination in Bacteria," it furthered knowledge of the structure and function of DNA—the molecules in each animal gene that through a complex series of chemical codes determine inherited physical makeup and characteristics.

President Truman was pleased with the progress of the NSF, and for the fiscal year 1953 he requested a huge increase in its budget—from $3.5 million

Max Delbrueck, a scientist at the California Institute of Technology,
prepares a petri dish for study under a microscope. In 1952,
Delbrueck received an NSF grant to conduct genetics research, which
later revealed new information about the structure of DNA.

to $15 million. But before Congress could decide on the matter, Dwight D. Eisenhower, a Republican, replaced Truman as president. Eisenhower was determined to wipe out a $10 billion federal budget deficit that had developed under Truman. He decided that science funding was one of the items that could be cut to balance the budget. Congress, which was controlled by the Republican party, acceded to his wishes, allotting only $8 million to the NSF for 1954.

Although Eisenhower slashed the NSF's budget, he did help clear up confusion about the agency's mission. During his first months in office, Congress held yet another set of discussions on the NSF. Many congressmen argued that the foundation should fund applied as well as basic research. Eisenhower issued an executive order that reaffirmed the NSF's commitment to basic research. The order made clear that the NSF should continue to evaluate research programs conducted by other federal departments and help the government define its role in science.

Entering the Space Age

In the late 1950s, the NSF expanded markedly as a consequence of the Soviet Union's launching of *Sputnik*, the first artificial satellite. The launching, which

Sputnik, *the first artificial satellite, launched by the Soviet Union in 1957. U.S. alarm at the Soviets' head start in developing space technology produced a groundswell of support from the public to increase funding for large-scale science projects and to improve science education in schools.*

52

A scientist at a research station in Antarctica launches a weather balloon to measure atmospheric conditions. In 1959, the NSF negotiated the Antarctic Treaty with 11 other nations to establish the continent as a nonmilitary, international scientific preserve.

took place in September 1957, shocked Americans, who had always considered their nation's technology and science to be far superior to those of the other superpower. Many were convinced that radical changes were needed in American science and education. Lawmakers agreed that federal funding of basic research had to be increased, and as a result, between 1957 and 1959, the NSF's budget ballooned from $40 million to $139 million. For the first time, the NSF began supporting big science projects. One of the earliest was a radio telescope observatory at Green Bank, West Virginia, which was set up under a $4 million contract with Associated Universities, Inc.—a nonprofit company formed by several colleges.

NSF educational programs also grew in the wake of the *Sputnik* launching. In 1958, Congress passed the National Defense Education Act, which allotted $900 million in federal aid for education in mathematics, science, and foreign languages. The NSF received a considerable share of this money. As one of its new activities, it began to support institutions that trained high school science teachers. It also sponsored the development of new curricula in the sciences.

Meanwhile, the foundation devoted increasing attention to promoting international scientific cooperation. It assigned several attachés (diplomats with expertise in a certain area) to American embassies to monitor scientific developments in foreign countries. It arranged for exchanges of scientists with other nations. The foundation also represented the United States in the International Geophysical Year (1956–57), an 18-month cooperative effort by 67 nations to study the earth and its cosmic surroundings. The NSF set up and funded several cooperative joint ventures in the fields of atmospheric, oceanographic, and ecological research. Toward the end of the Geophysical Year, the NSF negotiated an agreement with 11 other nations to establish a research center in Antarctica. A year later, these nations signed a treaty pledging to preserve the icy continent as a zone of peace.

At the end of the NSF's first decade, Waterman and the board finally decided to take advantage of the loophole in the charter that allowed for the funding of social sciences. But they agreed to fund only social sciences that were characterized by "objectivity, verifiability, and generality."

The 1960s: Expansion and Reorganization

During the 1960s, Presidents Kennedy and Lyndon B. Johnson convinced Congress to step up funding for the NSF. During his first months in office, Kennedy announced plans to send a man to the moon. A groundswell of support for Kennedy's initiative helped raise spending levels for all federal science agencies involved in astronomy and physics. Under Johnson, federal funds for basic research increased by 50 percent, whereas expenditures on research and development rose only 10 percent. By 1968, the NSF budget had increased to $500 million.

During this period, the foundation sponsored several new big science endeavors. For example, it funded and helped coordinate the Mohole project, an effort to increase understanding of the earth's composition by drilling through the mantle (the layer of rock covering the planet's core) from an offshore oil rig. In 1968, Congress disbanded the project, deciding that it cost too much. But in the meantime, the NSF had launched a second deep-sea drilling operation—this time using a research ship called the *Glomar Challenger*. Geological specimens retrieved by the ship from beneath the ocean floor helped to expand knowledge of plate tectonics—the field of study devoted to investigating the composition, movement, and interaction of the 12 or more plates into which the earth's crust is divided. Called the Deep Sea Drilling

On July 20, 1969, Apollo 11 *astronaut Edwin ("Buzz") Aldrin became the second man to walk on the moon (Commander Neil Armstrong was the first). During the lunar landing, Aldrin and Armstrong set up several scientific instruments, including a laser beam reflector, a seismometer (which later transmitted data about a moonquake), and a sheet of aluminum foil to trap solar wind.*

The NSF's research ship Glomar Challenger *was used to gather geological specimens from the ocean floor and to investigate the theory of continental drift. The project, launched in 1968, provided new evidence in support of the theory that the earth's continents may once have been a single land mass.*

Project, it also helped confirm the theory of continental drift—the hypothesis that movement of the plates has taken continents, once joined in a single landmass, farther and farther from each other.

Although these big science projects attracted the attention of the public, they remained less important to the NSF than support of research in the universities. In the 1960s, the foundation added a new wrinkle to its support for academic science. It began awarding grants not just to individual scientists but to entire university science departments. These new grants were of several types. Facility grants were awarded to schools that needed to build new

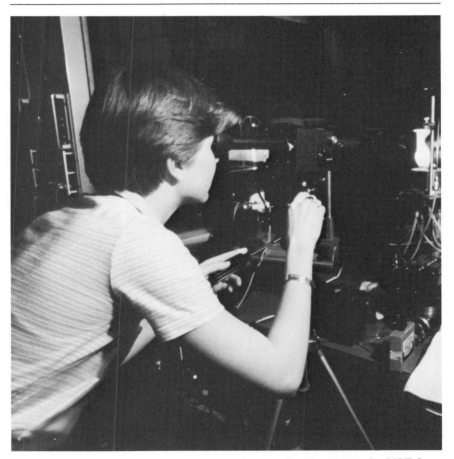

A graduate student peers into a microscope. In the 1960s the NSF began awarding grants to entire university science departments in addition to funding individual scientists.

research laboratories or refurbish old ones. Formula grants gave more than 1,000 colleges funds that could be used by college administrators to improve science programs in any way they saw fit—to pay for research, construct labs, buy supplies, or improve instruction. College science improvement grants were designated specifically to strengthen science classes for undergraduate students, and departmental development grants were awarded to individual departments.

During Kennedy's presidency, the NSF underwent some important institutional changes. Two of the tasks assigned to the NSF by its charter were coordinating federal science activities and developing a national science policy. Although the foundation was hugely successful in administering grants, it had problems performing these two duties. Managing federal science activities proved to be beyond the capacity of its administrative apparatus. NSF leaders were not interested in setting science policy. By the 1960s, Congress came to accept the notion that the NSF would never perform these two tasks. Under the Reorganization Act of 1962, the Office of Science and Technology was formed to take them over.

Waterman's second term expired, and he retired while Kennedy was still in office. He was replaced by Leland J. Haworth, a scientist with impressive credentials in science management. Having started his career as a university physics professor, Haworth worked on radiation research during World War II and afterward held several administrative posts in the sciences, including director of the Brookhaven National Laboratory, president of Associated Universities, Inc., and member of the board of directors of the Oak Ridge Institute for Nuclear Studies in Tennessee. Between 1961 and 1969, he served on the Atomic Energy Commission.

The Changes Continue

During Haworth's tenure, which lasted from 1963 to 1969, Congress revised the laws governing the NSF to reflect changes that had occurred in the agency since the act of 1950 was passed. The House Subcommittee on Science, Research, and Development, under Chairman Emilio Daddario, drew up a bill to amend the NSF charter. The bill, which was passed in 1968, gave explicit sanction to the foundation's practice of funding social sciences and created a separate division of social sciences. To assist the director in managing an expanding research budget and supervising an increasing number of programs, the bill created five new staff positions—a deputy director and four assistant

Emilio Daddario, chairman of the House Subcommittee on Science, Research, and Development, in 1968. Under Daddario's leadership, Congress passed a bill that created a separate division within the NSF to fund social science research and also enabled the NSF to begin funding applied research projects, such as the supersonic transport plane (SST).

directors. Recognizing the foundation's success in compiling and publishing information on the sciences, the bill asked the NSF to prepare an annual report on science policy issues. But the most significant provision of the bill called for the NSF to begin funding applied research along with basic research. This move was supported by both conservative congressmen who wanted NSF funds to go toward weapons development and liberal legislators who hoped the foundation would support research on environmental protection.

For his part, Haworth supported the NSF's foray into applied research, believing that it would make the agency more socially relevant. But he made

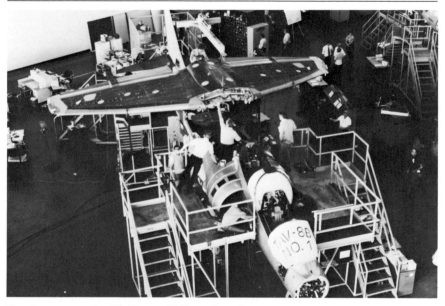

Engineers at the McDonnell Douglas Corporation in St. Louis, Missouri, work on improving a military aircraft. The NSF's second director, Leland J. Haworth, supported the move to increase emphasis on applied research in 1968 but made it clear that the NSF would predominantly fund basic research.

clear that the NSF's primary mission was still basic research. When Richard Nixon took office as president in 1969, he tried to increase emphasis on applied research. Haworth's successor, William D. McElroy (1969–72) was willing to back several applied research projects, but he did so only as a way of increasing congressional funding of the NSF. Ultimately, he managed to increase the foundation's commitment to basic research—as did his successors, H. Guyford Stever (1972–76), Richard C. Atkinson (1977–80), and John B. Slaughter (1980–86).

President Nixon also conducted a major overhaul of the federal science apparatus. He had become increasingly frustrated with the agencies assigned to help him formulate national science policy, the Office of Science and Technology and the office of the presidential science adviser. Leaders of those offices had openly criticized his conduct of the Vietnam War and opposed his plans to use federal funds to develop a new antiballistic missile system and a supersonic transport (a plane that could fly faster than the speed of sound). In January 1973, Nixon announced that, as of July 1, both offices would be abolished and the role of science adviser would be assumed by the director of the NSF.

The move elicited vehement protests from many of the nation's scientists, who felt they had been deprived of substantial influence in the higher echelons of the executive branch. Many believed that saddling the NSF with this new task would subject it to excessive political pressure and distract it from its primary purpose of funding research. Nevertheless, from 1973 to 1976, the NSF director served as the president's principal adviser on scientific affairs. The director at the time, H. Guyford Stever, set up a science and technology policy office within the foundation to assist him with his new duties. After Arab countries imposed an oil embargo on the United States during the 1973 Arab-Israeli War, this new office provided valuable counsel to the president on locating and developing domestic oil resources. It also helped arrange for extensive scientific exchanges with the Soviet Union.

When Gerald Ford became president in 1974, he sought to restore the science apparatus that Nixon had dismantled. He wanted to accomplish this through an act of Congress, not an executive order. After two years of negotiations, his wish came true—Congress established the new Office of Science and Technology Policy (OSTP) and designated its head as science adviser to the president. Stever was put in charge of the OSTP and was replaced as NSF director by Deputy Director Richard C. Atkinson, a psychologist. In the meantime, the foundation had become embroiled in a controversy over one of the many educational courses it had helped develop since 1957—"Man: A Course of Study," a social science class in human behavior for fifth-grade students. By 1975 the class was taught in 1,700 elementary schools in 47 states, but many conservative critics now contended that the class distorted basic family values. Led by John Conlan of Arizona, a group of congressmen tried to push through a law requiring all foundation projects to undergo a congressional review before receiving funding. The attempt failed but pointed up the NSF's continuing difficulty in maintaining independence while making funding decisions.

During Ford's presidency, skyrocketing inflation significantly diminished the real value of money disbursed by the NSF, even though funding levels remained constant. To make its budget go as far as possible, the NSF began to favor support of people over instruments and facilities. As a result, many institutions put off indefinitely the replacement of expensive equipment and the renovation of aging laboratories. By the time Ford left office, the decline in the quality of the nation's scientific instrumentation had become a serious problem.

During the 1970s, several acts of Congress and executive orders expanded

A whale dives into the ocean. In 1972, the NSF was given the responsibility of nominating scientists to the Marine Mammal Commission, an agency formed to enforce the Marine Mammal Protection Act, which protects sea mammals from harm.

the responsibilities of the NSF. Under the Marine Mammal Protection Act of 1972, which established regulations to protect such sea mammals as sea otters, whales, and seals from being captured or killed by anyone under U.S. jurisdiction, the NSF was asked to nominate scientists for the Marine Mammal Commission—an agency established to enforce the regulations. The Metric Conversion Act of 1975 declared that the federal policy would be to plan the increasing use of the metric system in the United States and called for the NSF to provide funds to educational research groups that were developing methods for teaching the metric system to precollege students. Executive Order 11287 empowered the NSF to assist members of the President's Committee on the National Medal of Science with administrative procedures during their award activities. And Executive Order 11490 called for the NSF to help mobilize civilian manpower in the event of a major natural disaster, a war, a health crisis, or some other emergency.

Under Carter and Reagan

Presidents Jimmy Carter and Ronald Reagan spoke frequently of their interest in the NSF and its primary mission, basic research. Carter, who was trained as an engineer, viewed the promotion of scientific research as an investment in the nation's future. Reagan valued the agency for different reasons—because it helped strengthen the national defense and helped the nation compete economically in an increasingly technological world. Carter coupled his professed fondness for the foundation with concrete action to provide real growth in NSF expenditures. Reagan, however, took steps in the opposite direction. Deciding that reducing the size of the federal government was more important than promoting scientific research, he slashed the NSF budget in 1981 and 1982. Especially hard hit were social sciences and science education, two areas that had always received a smaller share of funds than the physical and life sciences. Reagan administration officials believed that social science programs were expendable because, in their view, these disciplines did not benefit the American economy in the long run. They thought that education programs would be better run by state and local authorities. Only intense lobbying by the science board and the NSF director kept these two facets of NSF operations from being eliminated altogether.

After 1982, however, the Reagan administration advocated considerably greater expenditures for the NSF. As Carter had before him, Reagan paid particular attention to expanding engineering programs. For most of the foundation's history, engineering had received a disproportionately small share of NFS funds because most engineering activities were considered applied science. In the late 1970s, out of a desire to stimulate economic growth, Congress had considered establishing a separate National Engineering Foundation. The Carter administration headed off this move by making the NSF's small engineering division into a directorate—the highest level of NSF divisions. Under Reagan, the new engineering directorate was allotted substantial resources with which to establish and fund engineering research centers around the nation. By 1985, the directorate had helped set up six such centers, including a center for robotics systems at the University of California at Santa Barbara and a center for biotechnological process engineering at MIT.

During the Reagan and Carter years, NSF leaders changed frequently. Richard Atkinson, who had taken over for Stever in 1977, resigned in 1980 to take a job as chancellor of the University of California at San Diego. He was succeeded as NSF director by John B. Slaughter, who also left after two years to assume a university chancellorship. Edward A. Knapp, a physicist from Los Alamos National Laboratory, ran the NSF from 1982 to 1984 and then returned to Los Alamos. In September 1984, Erich Bloch, an engineer who had recently retired from an executive position at IBM, took over the leadership spot, becoming the first NSF director from the corporate community.

The dome of the Nicholas U. Mayall telescope at the Kitt Peak National Observatory near Tucson, Arizona. The observatory is one of several optical astronomy research centers funded by the NSF's Directorate for Mathematical and Physical Sciences.

FOUR

Administrative Structure

The NSF forms part of the executive branch of the federal government, but it is classified as an independent agency—that is, it is independent of the 14 departments whose secretaries are members of the president's cabinet. The foundation's internal organization has undergone significant changes since it was established in 1950. At the outset, there were only four divisions—medical research; mathematical, physical, and engineering sciences; biological services; and scientific personnel and education—each headed by an assistant director. The director's staff consisted merely of a general counsel and an assistant director for administration. The National Science Board was assisted by only one full-time employee, an executive secretary. Between 1950 and 1952, fewer than 20 people worked for the NSF. Today, the foundation is staffed by more than 1,150 employees and includes 8 directorates, 12 offices, and 38 divisions.

Still, the top level of the NSF's structure remains the same as that provided for by the National Science Foundation Act. The foundation continues to be run by a "two-headed" chief executive—the director and the National Science Board. It is difficult to define precisely how power is divided between the two heads, especially because no current or former NSF leaders have published reports on the subject. In theory, the board makes policy for the foundation and the director carries it out. Whereas the board must approve all new programs—such as new grant programs to support scientific education, new joint endeavors with foreign countries, and new contracts to set up national research centers—the director manages the day-to-day operation of the programs. There is, however, a great deal of overlap. The director is involved in making policy as a member of the science board. Similarly, the board participates in the execution of policy in the sense that it must approve many of the director's actions.

National Science Board

The National Science Board consists of the NSF director and 24 members appointed by the president with the advice and consent of the Senate. Board members are chosen from academia, private industry, and other government science agencies. Under the 1950 National Science Foundation Act, each member is required to have a record of distinguished service in one of the scientific disciplines, engineering, agriculture, education, or public affairs. In theory, the board is supposed to include an equal number of members from each geographic area of the country. In practice, the majority of positions have gone to scientists from the most prominent universities. In nominating members of the board, the president must, in the words of the 1950 act, "give due consideration to any recommendations for nomination which may be submitted to him by the National Academy of Sciences, the Association of Land Grant Colleges and Universities, the National Association of State Universities, the Association of American Colleges, and other scientific and educational organizations." The term of office for each board member is six years. Every two years, the terms of one-third of the members expire, and the president either replaces them or reappoints them. A member may serve only two consecutive terms, after which he or she must wait two years before being reappointed. Also, every two years the board elects a chairman and a vice-chairman. The chairman presides over all meetings and handles interactions with the NSF director between meetings. The vice-chairman takes over when the chairman is not available. Meetings are convened at least once a year, in May. Additional meetings may be held if the chairman so decides or if one-third of the board so requests in writing. On the average, the board meets about nine times a year. Members are paid $30 for each day they spend on NSF work.

Under the 1950 National Science Foundation Act, the board is permitted to elect an executive committee and delegate to it any powers or duties. The

In 1988, Mary L. Good, a highly regarded chemist and senior vice-president of technology at Allied-Signal Corporation in Des Plaines, Illinois, was appointed chairman of the 1988 National Science Board. The president chooses board members from academia, private industry, and other government science agencies, appointing them to six-year terms.

committee may have as many as nine members and no fewer than five, and it must include the NSF director. Most of the time, the executive committee has had five members. They are elected to two-year terms and may not serve more than three terms consecutively. The committee delivers an annual report to the board describing its activities. These reports are not available to the public.

The science board is assisted by a small staff of full-time federal employees, who are chosen by the NSF director and headed by an executive officer. As of 1987, there were five such employees. Their job is to gather background information for the board, arrange meetings, facilitate communication between members, and help prepare reports.

By law, the National Science Board is required to submit an annual report to Congress. Traditionally, however, this task has been handled by the director.

NSF Director

The director of the NSF is appointed by the president, subject to confirmation by the Senate. The National Science Board is authorized to suggest candidates for the director's position, and the president must consider these recommendations in making his selection. Before being considered by the Senate as a whole, the president's nominee is questioned first by the Labor and Public

Erich Bloch, a retired IBM executive, was appointed director of the NSF by President Ronald Reagan in 1984. Bloch is the first director to have come from private industry.

Welfare Committee (the Senate committee that deals with all legislative matters concerning the foundation). The 1950 National Science Foundation Act set the director's term at six years and stipulated that he could not serve more than two consecutive terms.

The director has many duties. The most important ones are providing day-to-day management of all NSF programs and supervising personnel. He is also in charge of relations with Congress, supplying information upon request and frequently appearing as a witness before congressional committees. He must attend all meetings of the National Science Board and its executive committee, over which he presides as chairman. He belongs to several presidential advisory boards, the Federal Council for Science and Technology, the Defense Science Board, and the President's Committee on Manpower. And he handles relations with other governmental science organizations, quasi-governmental agencies such as the National Academy of Sciences, private industry, and academia. The director is assisted in his managerial tasks by a deputy director, who takes over when the director is absent or has resigned. The deputy director is appointed by the director, with the approval of the board.

Directly below the foundation's two senior officials in the NSF structure are five offices that have staff functions. This means they do not themselves carry out foundation programs; instead they perform some function that helps the director carry out programs efficiently and properly. The Office of the General Counsel furnishes legal advice to the director and other foundation officials. The Office of Legislative and Public Affairs arranges for NSF officials to appear before congressional committees, conducts regular briefings for members of Congress on NSF activities, manages relations with the news media, and distributes publications that describe the foundation's history and its activities. The Office of Budget, Audit, and Control prepares the agency's budget and conducts routine audits and inspections of foundation programs to assess their effectiveness and identify their shortcomings. The Office of Information Systems manages the NSF's computer network. And the Office of Science and Technology Centers Development prepares plans for the NSF to establish and coordinate new research centers.

Directorates and Divisions

Beneath the staff offices and top officials in the NSF structure are the eight directorates, which are the main operating subdivisions of the foundation. The directorates employ most of the foundation's staff members and administer the vast majority of its programs. They review most of the funding proposals it receives, make most of the funding decisions, and control most of the budget. Because the NSF receives 28,000 to 32,000 proposals a year, the National Science Board and the NSF director cannot possibly review all of them; therefore, only grants involving a total of more than $6 million or an annual expenditure of more than $1.5 million actually come before the director and the board.

Each directorate is broken up into several smaller components called divisions, which are in turn broken up into programs. At the head of each directorate is an assistant director appointed by the NSF director. Assistant directors are responsible for running the divisions and programs in their respective directorates, preparing budget proposals for the programs under their jurisdiction, and defending their budget proposals before the Office of Management and Budget and Congress.

Five of the NSF directorates are engaged principally in running programs that provide grants for scientific research. These five are the Directorate for Biological, Behavioral, and Social Sciences; the Directorate for Computer and Information Science and Engineering; the Directorate for Engineering; the Directorate for Geosciences; and the Directorate for Mathematical and Physical Sciences. Each of these directorates distributes grants for several related scientific disciplines. For instance, the Directorate for Mathematical and Physical Sciences awards grants in mathematical sciences, physics, chemistry, astronomical sciences, and materials research. For each of the disciplines a directorate handles, it has a corresponding division. Within each division, there are several grant programs that deal with subcategories of the discipline. For example, within the Division of Physics, there are programs for such fields as theoretical physics, gravitational physics, particle physics, and intermediate engineering physics. The majority of grant decisions are made at the program level. Proposals that are somewhat more important than average are referred by the program head to the division director; proposals more significant than that go to the assistant director; and the most important ones go before the NSF director and the National Science Board. All five scientific research directorates administer grants for both little science and big science projects. The Division of Astronomical Sciences, for instance, not only distributes money for limited astronomical studies by individual researchers but also funds and oversees the major astronomical research centers that the NSF has helped set up over the years. Similarly, the Directorate of Geosciences, through its Division of Ocean Sciences, supported the 18-year ocean-drilling

Scientific researchers at work. Five of the eight NSF directorates devote their energies to funding scientific research in the following areas: biological, behavioral, and social sciences; computer and information science and engineering; engineering; geosciences; and mathematical and physical sciences.

project involving the ship *Glomar Challenger*, in addition to small laboratory studies.

The three other NSF directorates—the Directorate for Science and Engineering Education; the Directorate for Scientific, Technological, and International Affairs; and the Directorate for Administration—have very different functions. The Directorate for Science and Engineering Education administers all of the department's educational programs. It awards graduate fellowships, distributes grants to college science departments, funds educational researchers who develop new curricula and materials for precollege science education, and supports institutes that train precollege science teachers.

The Directorate for Scientific, Technological, and International Affairs, which includes five divisions and two offices, runs a variety of programs that fall

1988 Announcement

National Science Foundation
DIRECTORATE FOR SCIENCE AND ENGINEERING EDUCATION
Division of Research Career Development

NSF GRADUATE RESEARCH FELLOWSHIPS

GRADUATE FELLOWSHIPS

Apply to:
The Fellowship Office, National Research Council
2101 Constitution Avenue, Washington, D.C. 20418

OMB 3145-0058
PT 22.34
KW 0400000
 0600000
 1000000

Deadline for entering the competition: November 13, 1987

Announcement of Awards: Mid-March 1988

NSF 87-4

A flier announces NSF graduate research fellowships for the academic year 1988–89. The Directorate for Science and Engineering Education awards fellowships to students at or near the beginning of their graduate study.

A teacher at the Exploratorium Teacher Institute explains the concept of stationary waves to other science teachers. The Directorate for Science and Engineering Education funds institutes that help train precollege teachers.

outside the scope of the scientific research directorates and the education directorate. Its Division of Science Resources Studies collects, stores, and distributes a wealth of information on the sciences. Through frequent surveys, it maintains current data on scientific personnel—on the geographic distribution of scientists, on their total number, and on the number involved in each discipline. It also keeps statistics on the number of people entering the scientific profession every year and the amount of money being spent on each discipline by the federal government and private foundations or corporations.

An American researcher measures the flow of nutrients in the plants of a tropical rain forest near the borders of Brazil, Colombia, and Venezuela. The Directorate for Scientific, Technological, and International Affairs sponsors cooperative research projects with other countries.

The Division of International programs coordinates scientific exchanges with other nations; helps launch and fund international scientific projects; and represents the United States at international scientific conferences. The Division of Policy Research and Analysis prepares reports on long-range foundation planning by the National Science Board and the NSF director. The division's reports help NSF leaders keep abreast of important recent discoveries and identify the disciplines most in need of federal assistance. The Division of Industrial Science and Technological Innovation distributes grants to industrial and academic scientists for applied research that may lead to new products. The Division of Research Initiative and Improvement runs programs aimed at increasing the number of women, disabled people, and members of minority groups involved in scientific research. For example, it administers grants to science departments at minority colleges, such as Howard University in Washington, D.C., funds efforts to make laboratories accessible to people who are in wheelchairs, and sponsors visiting professorships for women in the sciences.

The Directorate for Administration performs all the NSF's administrative tasks except those dealt with by staff offices. Consisting of one office and four divisions, it handles financial management, distributes budgetary funds among NSF divisions, and deals with personnel functions such as hiring, firing, promotion, and management of health benefits. Through its Office of Equal Opportunity, the Administrative Directorate is responsible for increasing the number of women and minorities in the department.

The staffs of NSF directorates consist of two types of employees—career government workers who belong to the Civil Service and temporary employees called rotators. The latter are scientists and administrators who agree to leave their jobs in academia and private industry for one or two years of service with the NSF. Rotators help the NSF keep in touch with the latest developments in science. There is one problem with employing them, however—their unfamiliarity with standard procedures often limits NSF efficiency. To help minimize this difficulty, the NSF makes sure that at least one permanent employee is assigned to each program.

Advisory Committees and Peer Reviewers

The National Science Board, the director, the deputy director, the staff offices, the directorates, and the divisions constitute the primary components of the NSF structure. They are supplemented, however, by several additional structural mechanisms through which the NSF maintains close contact with and allows for input from the scientific community. These mechanisms have helped ease the fears of those who worried that the creation of the NSF would result in excessive government interference in science.

One way in which the scientific community plays an active part in NSF operations is through advisory committees, panels of privately employed scientists who meet several times a year to advise NSF officials on policy and procedures. Under the 1950 National Science Foundation Act, advisory committees were set up for each NSF division. The act spelled out precise rules for each committee, specifying the number of members on each and the length of members' terms. As the foundation grew, however, this arrangement proved to be too rigid: With the establishment of new divisions that often had overlapping responsibilities, NSF leaders recognized a need for committees that could deal with more than one division. Reorganization Plan No. 5 of 1965 abolished the original division of committees and authorized the director and his aides to establish advisory committees for any level of the foundation.

Under the current system, there are advisory committees attached to each division of the five scientific research directorates, several attached to directorates, and some responsible for individual programs. In 1988, there were 26 advisory committees. Members of each committee are appointed by the head of the body that they advise. So, for instance, the members of the Advisory Committee for the Directorate for Biological, Behavioral, and Social Sciences are chosen by the assistant director for Biological, Behavioral, and Social Sciences. The number of members on each committee varies from panel to panel, as does the length of members' terms. Among other duties, committees examine grant procedures, discuss areas of research to which the NSF should devote more attention, and look over recent grant approvals by NSF officials. Committees do not, however, approve grants themselves. Each committee provides the NSF director with an annual report, and each committee chairman gives an oral presentation to the National Science Board each year.

In addition to sitting on formal committees, private scientists help evaluate grant proposals for the NSF. For each proposal submitted to the NSF, the foundation hires a team of scientists to serve as outside experts, called peer reviewers or merit reviewers. The reviewers are chosen by program directors and serve without pay. (Being appointed to serve as a peer reviewer is considered quite prestigious, and, for most scientists, is payment in itself.) There are three different procedures by which a grant proposal is put before reviewers. Some proposals are sent by mail to reviewers, who prepare written evaluations and return them to the program director. For other proposals, the reviewers gather in Washington, D.C., to evaluate the proposal in person in a group discussion. Still other proposals are assessed by a combination of mail reviewers and panel reviewers.

Peer reviewers evaluate proposals on two bases—scientific merit and budget. They give each proposal a score from one to five in both categories. These evaluations are given to the program director, who uses them in deciding whether or not to fund a project. From 5 to 15 reviewers are asked to evaluate each proposal. Rarely is the same group of reviewers used for two proposals. Altogether, more than 36,000 scientists review proposals for the NSF every year.

Privately employed scientists also serve on special commissions that the foundation forms from time to time to conduct surveys of research in particular fields and to develop comprehensive research programs in these fields. In 1956, the NSF organized such a commission to investigate rubber research. And in 1964, it set up the Special Commission on Weather Modification.

The National Science Foundation Budget

The NSF budget for fiscal year 1987 was $1.9 billion. The largest share of the budget, $464.7 million, was spent on grants to support research in the mathematical and physical sciences. (Funding for physics totaled $117 million; for materials research, $108.9 million; for chemistry, $93.8 million; for astronomical sciences, $85.1 million; and for mathematical sciences, $59.9 million.) Geosciences received the next highest share, with $285.2 million ($133.7 million for ocean sciences, $93.4 million for atmospheric sciences, $49.9 million for earth sciences, and $8.109 million for arctic research). Biological, behavioral, and social sciences had the third-highest total, at $259.4 million ($58.3 million for biotic systems and resources, $44.2 million for molecular biosciences, $53.8 million for cellular biosciences, $43.3 million for behavioral and neural sciences, $28.6 million for instrumentation and re-sources, and $31.2 million for social and economic sciences). Of the 2 other scientific disciplines supported by the NSF, engineering grants totaled $163 million and computer sciences $116.9 million.

The NSF spent $99 million on educational programs in fiscal year 1987. Funding for industrial science and technology came to $16.8 million. And the budget for international scientific cooperation was $10.3 million.

The location of NSF headquarters in Washington, D.C., has grown progressively larger over the years: The agency began its operations in a residential building on 16th and I streets, NW (top left); then moved in 1951 to 2144 California Street, NW (top right). After a move to the former Cosmos Club at H Street and Madison Place, NW, in 1953, the agency expanded even more and in 1958 had to relocate to 1951 Constitution Avenue (bottom left); in 1965, the NSF moved to its present location at 1800 G Street, NW (bottom right).

Facilities

During its history, the NSF has had several homes. For government office spaces, most of these have been unusually distinctive. In its first year, 1950, the foundation set up its headquarters in a three-story brick residential building on 16th and I streets in Washington, D.C. The first NSF director, Alan Waterman, described the building as "not quite old enough to be antique, but not quite young enough to boast any modern appurtenances." In 1951, to accommodate its growing staff, the NSF moved to a building on California Street that had formerly served as a private school. The structure consisted of four buildings that had been joined together in odd ways. In 1953, as the staff continued to grow, the NSF relocated to a group of buildings that had once been a men's club and hotel called the Cosmos Club. By 1958, however, expansion spurred on by the *Sputnik* launching compelled the NSF to move once again, this time to a more traditional office space on Constitution Avenue. Many officials welcomed the move because it put the NSF near the National Academy of Sciences. But others missed the character of the earlier buildings. As one official said, "The California Street building was not efficient from an office point of view, but it was nice to work in. . . . It adds something sort of special if you're not just walking down a government corridor with lots of green walls."

In 1965, the NSF moved to a 12-story office building on G Street in northwest Washington, D.C., where today it occupies 6 floors. The vast majority of its employees work in this office, but a few staffers involved in science resource programs are stationed in a building on M Street. Because most NSF employees are involved in paperwork, the agency needs much less space than government science agencies that conduct their own research.

A math teacher explains an assignment to his students. One part of the NSF's mission is to help educate precollege science teachers and to enrich the learning process by effectively preparing them to serve as models to their students.

FIVE

The NSF's Mission

The mission of the NSF is to promote the progress of science. The primary means by which it fulfills this assignment is by funding the research projects of academic scientists. But it also performs several other important functions: funding national research centers, supporting science education, promoting international scientific cooperation, aiding industrial scientific research, and conferring national science awards. The foundation's support of science plays an important role in the economic development of the country. Basic research funded by the NSF generates much of the new knowledge that eventually results in innovative products, better health care, new jobs in a growing economy, and a strong national defense.

Supporting Scientific Research

The NSF will consider proposals for research in almost any field of science, including astronomy, atmospheric sciences, biological and behavioral sciences, chemistry, computer sciences, earth sciences, engineering, information science, materials research, mathematical sciences, oceanography, physics, and social sciences. Some research projects, however, are specifically excluded

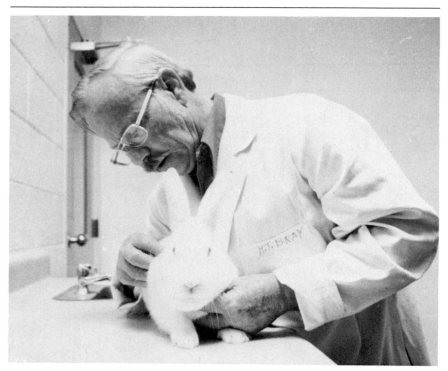

A scientist checks a rabbit during an experiment. The NSF does not fund projects involving the testing of drugs on laboratory animals.

from NSF funding: projects requiring security classification, those involving laboratory animals, projects developing products for commercial marketing, and those involving clinical research (defined in the NSF's *Guide to Programs, 1988* as "research on the etiology, diagnosis, or treatment of physical or mental disease, abnormality, or malfunction in human beings"). Once the NSF awards funds to a project, it ceases to play a role: It is not involved in the conduct of any research and takes no responsibility for the interpretations or conclusions of the studies that it funds.

Little Science

From the beginning, the NSF has placed particular emphasis on supporting little science—limited research projects—as opposed to the big science being done by national research centers and national research programs. At the outset, this decision reflected the small size of early appropriations: The NSF could not afford to bankroll major projects. But today, even though the budget has grown tremendously, the focus on little science endures. The method by which individual researchers obtain NSF money is called the project grant method. It works in the following manner. A researcher who wants to be considered by the NSF as a potential recipient of funding must prepare and submit a written description of the proposed research project. Proposals are accepted from researchers affiliated with universities, colleges, nonprofit organizations, and small businesses. (Funding for those associated with educational institutions usually takes precedence over commercial research because companies have access to funding from the private sector.) Proposals may be submitted by individual scientists or groups of scientists. Applicants may ask for money not only to fund the research but to pay salaries for assistants and to purchase equipment.

Most proposals that the NSF concerns itself with are submitted by a researcher on his or her own initiative—without the NSF asking for the research to be done. Unsolicited proposals, if accepted, are often supported on the condition that the researcher's organization share part of the cost. A small portion of grant proposals are solicited by the NSF; these grant projects, if approved, are paid for in full by the foundation.

Grant proposals must be organized in a specific format prescribed by the NSF. Applicants may obtain guidelines on this format from the NSF office or from several science organizations around the nation. The cover page of the proposal must provide a general summary of the research to be conducted and list the major investigators. In the body of the proposal, the applicant must give a detailed description of the work to be undertaken, outlining why the results will be important to the future of scientific knowledge and demonstrating an understanding of the previous work done in the field. It must also include a short biographical sketch of each principal research scientist and a list of previous publications. This information helps the NSF determine whether the applicants have adequate background in the proposed field of inquiry.

One of the most important aspects of the proposal is a detailed accounting of how funds will be used. Research work often costs a great deal of money, especially those projects that are at the forefront of technology. The proposal must state how much money will be spent on wages, new equipment, travel, and publication of the results of the study. (Usually wages are the biggest expense; however, on some technology-intensive projects, equipment takes the largest share of the budget.)

Additional information is required in a few special cases. Proposals for many outdoor projects calculate the impact the project will have on the environment.

Proposals for research in foreign countries must show why researchers in those countries cannot conduct the project themselves. Special justification is also required for research involving the use of human subjects, hazardous materials, laboratory animals, marine mammals, or endangered species.

When the proposal is completed by the researcher, he or she sends the necessary papers to the corresponding scientific directorate. The director of the directorate forwards the proposal to the correct division. For example, proposals involving oceanography are sent to the Directorate for Geosciences, which passes them along to the Division of Ocean Sciences.

Within the division, the proposal is given to the director who oversees the grant program from which funding is sought. First, the program director checks to make sure there is nothing lacking from the proposal or that needs further explanation. If there is, he or she will contact the researcher to make changes in the proposal before proceeding to the next stage in the process. (On rare occasions, the program director rejects the proposal outright.) Next, the proposal is sent to reviewers. When all of the evaluations from reviewers have been received, the proposal is sent back to the program director. The director weighs all of the reviewers' comments and either makes a decision or forwards the proposal to the next level—the division director. In most cases, if the reviewers recommend rejecting the proposal, the program director follows their lead. In some cases, in which there is a dispute among NSF officials, a partial grant may be awarded in order to see if the research is really worth funding in the future.

Proposals are usually judged two times a year, and funding is provided for accepted proposals during the next financial year; those researchers whose proposals have been rejected may revise their papers and submit them for the following review period. At the conclusion of NSF-funded projects, the researchers publish their results. All of these studies are made public, and anyone in the country may obtain them by contacting the NSF or the researcher.

Big Science

In addition to backing research efforts by individual scientists, the NSF annually provides money to several major research centers around the country and supports a number of large-scale, long-term research projects. These centers and projects are referred to as big science. Unlike little science projects, they run indefinitely, so they are funded through contracts rather than grants. A number of the research centers supported by the NSF were founded by the

A radio telescope at the National Radio Astronomy Observatory in Green Bank, West Virginia. The observatory, constructed in 1956, was the first big science project in astronomy that the NSF helped to establish.

agency. Under the NSF charter, however, the foundation is prohibited from actually operating the centers.

The majority of big science projects funded by the NSF are in the geosciences and astronomy. The first center that the NSF helped to establish was the National Radio Astronomy Observatory at Green Bank, West Virginia. It was set up in 1956 under a contract with the NSF. In subsequent years, the NSF helped set up two additional radio astronomy centers—the Very Large Array, west of Socorro, New Mexico (where 27 radio telescopes search the skies for radio waves), and the National Astronomy and Ionosphere Center at Cornell University in Ithaca, New York. The center at Cornell is in charge of running and analyzing the data from a huge 305-meter radio/radar telescope in Arecibo, Puerto Rico, which is the world's largest single radio reflector.

The NSF also funds the most prominent optical astronomy research center in the United States, the National Optical Astronomy Observatories (NOAO), which has headquarters in Tucson, Arizona. NOAO has several observatories around the nation, including Kitt Peak National Observatory in Arizona and the

The Very Large Array, west of Socorro, New Mexico, consists of 27 antennae and was set up by the NSF as a radio astronomy center.

National Solar Observatory (which has observing facilities atop Kitt Peak and at Sacramento Peak, New Mexico), where researchers study the various stars and galaxies of the universe.

In the geosciences, centers funded by the NSF include the National Center for Atmospheric Research (NCAR) in Boulder, Colorado. Researchers at NCAR study the physical composition of the atmosphere and the oceans and operate special facilities for solar astronomy research. Another geoscience organization funded by the NSF is the Upper Atmospheric Facilities—a network of radar centers located along a geographic line stretching from Greenland to Peru; they are used to determine the structure and dynamics of the earth's upper atmosphere.

The NSF has also joined with a coalition of universities and private companies around the nation to coordinate and fund a group of research centers that are developing advanced computers called supercomputers. These research centers are called National Supercomputer Centers. The five supercomputer centers are at the University of Pittsburgh, the University of San Diego, the University of Illinois at Champaign/Urbana, the John von Neumann Center near Princeton University, and Cornell University.

The solar telescope at Sacramento Peak Observatory, Sunspot, New Mexico. The NSF supports this optical astronomy center, where researchers can observe the detailed structure of planetary surfaces and the solar system.

The supercomputer center at the University of Pittsburgh in Pennsylvania. With such state-of-the-art computers, scientists and engineers can quickly process information and work on problems that were once thought to be impossible to resolve.

The supercomputers are five state-of-the-art computers that will be linked to each other via special telecommunication networks. They enable scientists to solve in a few hours complex mathematical equations that without advanced computing capabilities take hundreds or even thousands of hours to solve.

The researchers who work at the centers are all selected on the basis of their research proposals. For example, an astronomer who wants to study the field of radio astronomy at the Arecibo radio telescope in Puerto Rico (a center funded by the NSF) sends a proposal to the foundation; if his or her research grant is approved (the proposal goes through the same approval procedure as a project grant), the scientist will work, for a predetermined period of time, at the radio telescope.

Funding Education

The NSF supports many educational programs, from studies in the classroom to television programs. It administers programs that provide laboratory equipment to colleges and that develop science materials for precollege classrooms. It also sponsors a number of scientific educational programs conducted by museums, clubs, and other organizations.

In addition, the NSF supports National Science and Technology Week (formerly National Science Week), held each May in several communities across the country. The program is designed to boost public awareness of

The NSF supported an award-winning television program, "Mathematics 'R' Us," in the mid-1980s in an effort to interest schoolchildren in science and mathematics.

science and engineering and to encourage elementary, junior, and senior high school students to study science.

The NSF, in partnership with professional societies, educators, community organizations, and industries, explains science to the general public in a multitude of ways during National Science and Technology Week. Some groups have science fairs for young people. At art museums and libraries famous scientists give lectures, and exhibits and special science collections are displayed.

During past National Science and Technology Weeks, many communities were involved in different activities. For example, in Washington, D.C., 200,000 balloons were launched carrying weather cards—postcards that were to be filled out and returned by the finder of the balloon. In this way, scientists and students discover how the path of winds in the atmosphere carries the

Karen S. Ward, a teacher at Lincoln Southeast High School, Lincoln, Nebraska, received a Presidential Award for Excellence in Mathematics Teaching in 1987. The NSF gives these awards to each state's two most outstanding teachers in math and science.

balloons away. In Philadelphia, the Academy of Natural Sciences, along with other science organizations, sponsored the National Dinosaur Art Contest, giving students the chance to learn about the largest animals that ever lived on the earth.

Awards

To add incentive for quality work in science, the foundation offers a multitude of awards to teachers and researchers. Each year, in cooperation with the National Education Association (formerly the National Teachers Association), the NSF gives out Presidential Awards for Excellence in Science and Mathematics Teaching to two outstanding teachers in math and science from each state. These awards provide each recipient with a $5,000 grant for materials and training.

The Presidential Young Investigator Award is a monetary grant given to 200 of the nation's most outstanding and promising young professors in science and engineering. The Vannevar Bush Award recognizes individuals who have made an important contribution to public service activities in science and engineering. And the Alan T. Waterman Award is granted to a researcher who has earned a doctoral degree, is under 35 years of age, and shows innovation and excellence in his or her scientific research.

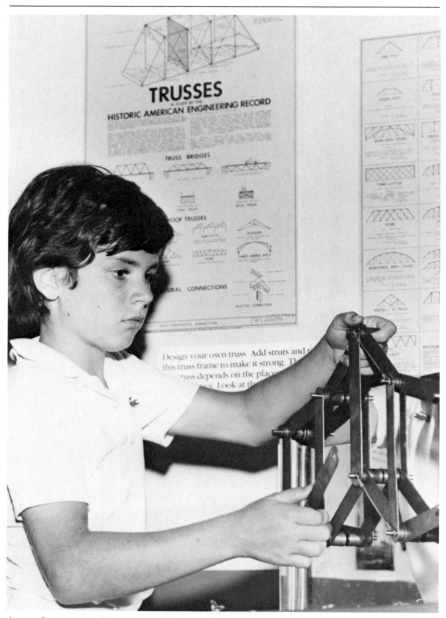

A student experiments with a model of a truss that illustrates how supports are used in such structures as bridges and roofs. The NSF continues to fund education programs that will spark interest in science and engineering.

SIX

Investment in the Future

The NSF has had a profound effect on the United States and the world. Thousands of research grants have been awarded to scientists, engineers, and mathematicians involved in basic research since the NSF was established in 1950. To meet the challenge of international competition in today's highly technological world, the NSF must continue to take the lead in maintaining a vigorous, well-supported, and well-equipped group of scientists and engineers to advance knowledge in the United States as well as abroad.

The NSF must also help to train future scientists and engineers. Other nations are witnessing a significant increase in the number of people entering the fields of science and engineering. During the 1980s in the United States, the number of college freshmen intending to major in science or engineering decreased by almost 30 percent because of greater interest in other fields. Only about 7 out of every 1,000 American students receive a degree in engineering, whereas in Japan, for example, 40 out of every 1,000 students graduate with degrees in engineering.

The NSF must continue to support education programs that will spark an interest in science, especially through its awards and research centers. Increased funding for scientific instruments and equipment in schools, colleges,

Children in a classroom explore the behavior of crayfish. The NSF offers funds to schools for instructional materials to help draw students into the world of science.

and universities will also help to extend the NSF's efforts to draw students into the world of science.

Scientific equipment itself must be updated to keep up with the changing needs of basic research. The NSF will continue to reinvest in research in order to improve instrumentation and laboratory facilities that—along with researchers—are the vital elements of the science and technology initiative.

International cooperation will continue to be encouraged by the NSF. Science, after all, is international by nature—investigation into the origin of the universe or the structure of the atom has no national borders. One recent NSF effort to increase international cooperation is a project called Global Geosciences. It is the United States's first large-scale funded program for multidiscipline cooperative studies and will eventually include collaboration with several other countries around the world. The scientists participating in Global Geosciences will examine both the natural changes in the world and the ways in which humans influence their world. To perform this study, they need to analyze the world as a single system—that is, simultaneously examine the atmosphere, oceans, continents, forms of life, and the ways in which all of these are linked. The Global Geosciences project stems from the recognition that a change in one system causes a change in another. By-products of human activity, such as the exhaust of automobiles, and natural processes, for example, may increase the amounts of carbon dioxide in the air. This increase can change the atmosphere, creating what is called the greenhouse effect. The result is a slow rise in atmospheric temperature that could gradually lead to the melting of ice in Antarctica, which, in turn, could cause sea levels to rise. The NSF works together with other federal agencies to support researchers and instruments that are located on the ground, under the ocean, and in the atmosphere to study such phenomena as the greenhouse effect.

The NSF will also need to defend its efforts in the future, especially when it is involved in controversy. Some universities, for example, frustrated with the NSF grant procedures, have bypassed the NSF's merit review process and have gone directly to Congress to request financial aid. The NSF believes that this action sets a dangerous precedent. NSF officials maintain that the merit review process is the best way to guarantee excellence in the science projects that are funded. With this type of review, the value of the research is explored and defined by a multitude of scientists and engineers who know which projects should have top priority in the United States.

Another controversial issue confronting the NSF today is its status in the government. Some officials and scientists want to see the NSF become a cabinet-level department within the executive branch. Others think that the NSF would suffer if it were to be pushed into higher levels of government.

Federal budgetary cuts will also force the NSF to choose projects to fund with greater care. More emphasis will be placed on cross-disciplinary research, showing how one subject may greatly affect another. The NSF has a firm foundation upon which to build and grow. Erich Bloch, director of the NSF during much of the 1980s, summed up the NSF's role in the nation's quest to be at the forefront of scientific discovery when he said, "The National Science Foundation has grown in breadth and responsibility, responding to the challenges arising from the search for new knowledge and from the importance of basic research to some of the Nation's primary concerns: quality of life, health, economic competitiveness, and national security."

The National Science Foundation

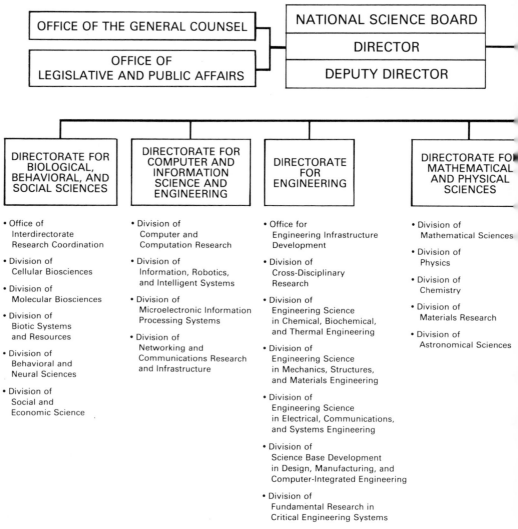

OFFICE OF THE GENERAL COUNSEL	NATIONAL SCIENCE BOARD
	DIRECTOR
OFFICE OF LEGISLATIVE AND PUBLIC AFFAIRS	DEPUTY DIRECTOR

DIRECTORATE FOR BIOLOGICAL, BEHAVIORAL, AND SOCIAL SCIENCES	DIRECTORATE FOR COMPUTER AND INFORMATION SCIENCE AND ENGINEERING	DIRECTORATE FOR ENGINEERING	DIRECTORATE FOR MATHEMATICAL AND PHYSICAL SCIENCES

DIRECTORATE FOR BIOLOGICAL, BEHAVIORAL, AND SOCIAL SCIENCES

- Office of Interdirectorate Research Coordination
- Division of Cellular Biosciences
- Division of Molecular Biosciences
- Division of Biotic Systems and Resources
- Division of Behavioral and Neural Sciences
- Division of Social and Economic Science

DIRECTORATE FOR COMPUTER AND INFORMATION SCIENCE AND ENGINEERING

- Division of Computer and Computation Research
- Division of Information, Robotics, and Intelligent Systems
- Division of Microelectronic Information Processing Systems
- Division of Networking and Communications Research and Infrastructure

DIRECTORATE FOR ENGINEERING

- Office for Engineering Infrastructure Development
- Division of Cross-Disciplinary Research
- Division of Engineering Science in Chemical, Biochemical, and Thermal Engineering
- Division of Engineering Science in Mechanics, Structures, and Materials Engineering
- Division of Engineering Science in Electrical, Communications, and Systems Engineering
- Division of Science Base Development in Design, Manufacturing, and Computer-Integrated Engineering
- Division of Fundamental Research in Critical Engineering Systems
- Division of Fundamental Research in Emerging Engineering Technology

DIRECTORATE FOR MATHEMATICAL AND PHYSICAL SCIENCES

- Division of Mathematical Sciences
- Division of Physics
- Division of Chemistry
- Division of Materials Research
- Division of Astronomical Sciences

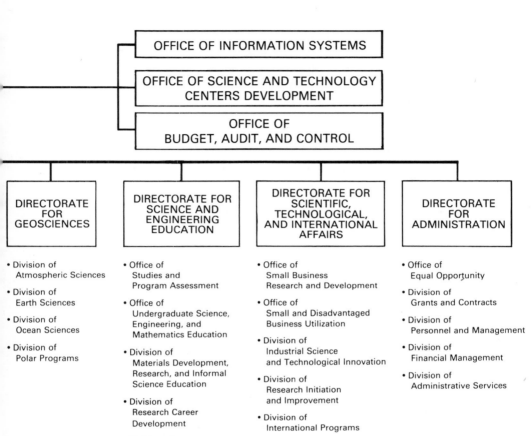

OFFICE OF INFORMATION SYSTEMS

OFFICE OF SCIENCE AND TECHNOLOGY
CENTERS DEVELOPMENT

OFFICE OF
BUDGET, AUDIT, AND CONTROL

| DIRECTORATE FOR GEOSCIENCES | DIRECTORATE FOR SCIENCE AND ENGINEERING EDUCATION | DIRECTORATE FOR SCIENTIFIC, TECHNOLOGICAL, AND INTERNATIONAL AFFAIRS | DIRECTORATE FOR ADMINISTRATION |

- Division of
  Atmospheric Sciences

- Division of
  Earth Sciences

- Division of
  Ocean Sciences

- Division of
  Polar Programs

- Office of
  Studies and
  Program Assessment

- Office of
  Undergraduate Science,
  Engineering, and
  Mathematics Education

- Division of
  Materials Development,
  Research, and Informal
  Science Education

- Division of
  Research Career
  Development

- Division of
  Teacher Preparation
  and Enhancement

- Office of
  Small Business
  Research and Development

- Office of
  Small and Disadvantaged
  Business Utilization

- Division of
  Industrial Science
  and Technological Innovation

- Division of
  Research Initiation
  and Improvement

- Division of
  International Programs

- Division of
  Policy Research
  and Analyses

- Division of
  Science Resource Studies

- Office of
  Equal Opportunity

- Division of
  Grants and Contracts

- Division of
  Personnel and Management

- Division of
  Financial Management

- Division of
  Administrative Services

97

GLOSSARY

Antiballistic missile   A missile used to intercept and destroy incoming warheads.

Archipelago   A group of islands.

Biotic   Of or relating to life.

Ecology   A branch of science concerned with the interrelationship of organisms and their environments.

Etiology   A branch of medical science concerned with the causes and origins of diseases.

Genealogy   An account of the descent of a person, family, or group from an ancestor.

Independent Agency   A government agency that is not subordinate to another federal agency or bureau.

National Science Board   The 24-member panel of scientists and educators who meet several times each year to formulate National Science Foundation policy.

Seismometer   An apparatus to measure the actual movements of the ground.

Vulcanologist   A scientist who studies volcanic phenomena.

SELECTED REFERENCES

Bush, Vannevar. *Science—The Endless Frontier: A Report to the President.* Washington, D.C.: U.S. Government Printing Office, 1945. Reprinted by the National Science Foundation in 1960 and 1980.

England, J. M. *A Patron for Pure Science: The National Science Foundation's Formative Years, 1945–57.* Washington, D.C.: National Science Foundation, 1982.

Lomask, Milton. *A Minor Miracle: An Informal History of the National Science Foundation.* Washington, D.C.: National Science Foundation, 1976.

Mazuzan, George. *The National Science Foundation: A Brief History.* Washington, D.C.: National Science Foundation, n.d.

National Science Foundation. *Annual Report.* Washington, D.C.: U.S. Government Printing Office. Issued every year since 1952.

————. *Guide to Programs, FY 1988.* Washington, D.C.: U.S. Government Printing Office, 1987.

Penick, J. L., et al. *The Politics of American Science: 1939 to the Present.* Cambridge, MA: MIT Press, 1972.

Reagan, Michael D. *Science and the Federal Patron.* New York: Oxford University Press, 1969.

Ronayne, J. *Science in Government: A Review of Principles and Practice of Science Policy.* Caulfield East, Australia: Edward Arnold, 1984.

Schaffter, Dorothy. *The National Science Foundation.* New York: Praeger, 1969.

Shannon, J. A. *Science and the Evolution of Public Policy.* New York: Rockefeller University Press, 1973.

Wolfe, Dael. "National Science Foundation: The First Six Years," *Science* 126 (August 1957): 335–43.

INDEX

Patricia L. Barnes-Svarney is a New York free-lance writer whose work has appeared in numerous scientific journals and publications, including *Water Resources Research, Rock and Gem,* and *Earth Science.* She has also worked as a physical oceanographer, geochemical analyst, and geological consultant. She holds a B.A. in geology from Catawba College, Salisbury, North Carolina, and an M.A. in physical geography from the State University of New York at Binghamton.

Arthur M. Schlesinger, jr., served in the White House as special assistant to Presidents Kennedy and Johnson. He is the author of numerous acclaimed works in American history and has twice been awarded the Pulitzer Prize. He taught history at Harvard College for many years and is currently Albert Schweitzer Professor of the Humanities at the City College of New York.